COTTAGE POEMS

By

PATRICK BRONTË

Including Introductory Essays by
Virginia Woolf and Clement K. Shorter

First published in 1811

Published by Ragged Hand,
an imprint of Read & Co.

Cottage Poems first published in 1811
This edition published by Read & Co. in 2018

Extra material © 2018 Read & Co. Books

All rights reserved. No portion of this book may be reproduced in any form without the permission of the publisher in writing.

A catalogue record for this book is available from the British Library.

ISBN: 9781528703840

Cover Design: Zoë Horn-Haywood

Read & Co. is part of Read Books Ltd.
For more information visit www.readandcobooks.co.uk

CONTENTS

PATRICK BRONTË AND MARIA HIS WIFE
By Clement K. Shorter 5

HAWORTH: NOVEMBER 1904
By Virginia Woolf 29

COTTAGE POEMS

EPISTLE TO THE REV. J--- B---, WHILST JOURNEYING FOR
THE RECOVERY OF HIS HEALTH 33

THE HAPPY COTTAGERS 39

THE RAINBOW 48

WINTER-NIGHT MEDITATIONS 53

VERSES SENT TO A LADY ON HER BIRTHDAY 61

THE IRISH CABIN 64

TO THE REV. J. GILPIN, ON HIS IMPROVED EDITION
OF THE "PILGRIM'S PROGRESS." 71

THE COTTAGE MAID 74

THE SPIDER AND THE FLY 79

EPISTLE TO A YOUNG CLERGYMAN 82

EPISTLE TO THE LABOURING POOR 86

THE COTTAGER'S HYMN 90

PATRICK BRONTË AND MARIA HIS WIFE

By Clement K. Shorter

It would seem quite clear to any careful investigator that the Reverend Patrick Brontë, Incumbent of Haworth, and the father of three famous daughters, was a much maligned man. We talk of the fierce light which beats upon a throne, but what is that compared to the fierce light which beats upon any man of some measure of individuality who is destined to live out his life in the quiet of a country village—in the very centre, as it were, of 'personal talk' and gossip not always kindly to the stranger within the gate? The view of Mr. Brontë, presented by Mrs. Gaskell in the early editions of her biography of Charlotte Brontë, is that of a severe, ill-tempered, and distinctly disagreeable character. It is the picture of a man who disliked the vanities of life so intensely, that the new shoes of his children and the silk dress of his wife were not spared by him in sudden gusts of passion. A stern old ruffian, one is inclined to consider him. His pistol-shooting rings picturesquely, but not agreeably, through Mrs. Gaskell's memoirs. It has been already explained in more than one quarter that this was not the real Patrick Brontë, and that much of the unfavourable gossip was due to the chatter of a dismissed servant, retailed to Mrs. Gaskell on one of her missions of inquiry in the neighbourhood. The stories of the burnt shoes and the mutilated dress have been relegated to the realm of myth, and the pistol-shooting may now be acknowledged as a harmless pastime not more iniquitous than the golfing or angling of a latter-day clergyman. It is certain, were the matter of much interest to-day, that Mr. Brontë was fond of the use of firearms. The present Incumbent of Haworth will point out to you, on the old tower of Haworth Church, the marks of pistol bullets, which he is assured were made by Mr. Brontë. I have myself handled both the gun and the pistol—this latter a very ornamental weapon, by the way, manufactured at Bradford—which Mr. Brontë possessed during the later years of his life. From both he had obtained much innocent amusement; but his son-in-law, Mr. Nicholls, who, at the distance of forty years still cherishes a reverent and enthusiastic affection for old Mr. Brontë, informs me that the bullet marks upon Haworth Church were the irresponsible frolic of a rather juvenile curate—Mr. Smith. All this is trivial enough in any case, and one turns very readily to more important factors in the life of the father of the Brontës. Patrick Brontë was born at Ahaderg, County Down, in Ireland, on St. Patrick's Day, March 17, 1777. He was one of the ten children of Hugh Brunty, farmer, and his nine brothers and sisters seem all of them to have spent their lives in their Irish home, to have married and been given in marriage, and to have gone to their graves in peace. Patrick alone had ambition, and, one must add, the opportune friend, without whom ambition counts for little in the great struggle of life. At sixteen he was a kind of village schoolmaster, or assistant schoolmaster, and at twenty-five, stirred thereto by the vicar of his parish, Mr. Tighe, he was on his way from Ireland to St. John's College, Cambridge. It was in 1802 that Patrick Brontë went to Cambridge, and entered his name in the college books. There, indeed, we find the name, not of Patrick Brontë, but of Patrick Branty,* and this brings us to an interesting point as to the origin of the name. In the register of his birth his name is entered, as are the births of his brothers and sisters, as 'Brunty' and 'Bruntee'; and it can scarcely be doubted that, as Dr. Douglas Hyde has pointed out, the original name was O'Prunty.† The Irish, at the beginning of the century, were well-nigh as primitive in some matters as were the English of a century earlier; and one is not surprised to see variations in the spelling of the Brontë name—it being in the case of his brothers and sisters occasionally spelt 'Brontee.' To me it is perfectly clear that for the change of name Lord Nelson was responsible, and that the dukedom of Brontë, which was conferred upon the great sailor in 1799, suggested the more ornamental surname. There were no Irish Brontës in existence before Nelson became Duke of Brontë; but all Patrick's brothers and sisters, with whom, it must be remembered, he was on terms of correspondence his whole life long, gradually, with a true Celtic sense of the picturesqueness of the thing, seized upon the more attractive surname. For this theory there is, of course, not one scrap of evidence; we only know that the register of Patrick's native parish gives us Brunty, and that his signature

---

* 'Patrick Branty' is written in another handwriting in the list of admissions at St. John's College, Cambridge. Dr. J. A. Erskine Stuart, who has a valuable note on the subject in an article on 'The Brontë Nomenclature' (Brontë Society's Publications, Pt. III.), has found the name as Brunty, Bruntee, Bronty, and Branty—but never in Patrick Brontë's handwriting. There is, however, no signature of Mr. Brontë's extant prior to 1799.

† 'I translated this' (i.e. an Irish romance) 'from a manuscript in my possession made by one Patrick O'Prunty, an ancestor probably of Charlotte Brontë, in 1763.' The Story of Early Gaelic Literature, p. 49. By Douglas Hyde, LL.D. T. Fisher Uwin, 1895.

through his successive curacies is Brontë.

From Cambridge, after taking orders in 1806, Mr. Brontë moved to a curacy at Weatherfield in Essex; and Mr. Augustine Birrell has told us, with that singular literary charm of his, how the good-looking Irish curate made successful love to a young parishioner—Miss Mary Burder. Mary Burder would have married him, it seems, but for an obdurate uncle and guardian. She was spirited away from the neighbourhood, and the lovers never met again. There are doubtful points in Mr. Birrell's story. Mary Burder, as the wife of a Nonconformist minister, died in 1866, in her seventy-seventh year. This lady, from whom doubtless either directly or indirectly the tradition was obtained, may have amplified and exaggerated a very innocent flirtation. One would like further evidence for the statement that when Mr. Brontë lost his wife in 1821 he asked his old sweetheart, Mary Burder, to become the mother of his six children, and that she answered 'no'. In any case, Mr. Brontë left Weatherfield in 1809 for a curacy at Dewsbury, and Dewsbury gossip also had much to say concerning the flirtations of its Irish curate. His next curacy, however, which was obtained in 1811, by a removal to Hartshead, near Huddersfield, brought flirtation for Mr. Brontë to a speedy end. In 1812, when thirty-three years of age, he married Miss Maria Branwell, of Penzance. Miss Branwell had only a few months before left her Cornish home for a visit to an uncle in Yorkshire. This uncle was a Mr. John Fennell, a clergyman of the Church of England, who had been a Methodist minister. To Methodism, indeed, the Cornish Branwells would seem to have been devoted at one time or another, for I have seen a copy of the *Imitation* inscribed 'M. Branwell, July 1807,' with the following title-page:—

> AN EXTRACT OF THE CHRISTIAN'S PATTERN: OR, A TREATISE ON THE IMITATION OF CHRIST. Written in Latin by Thomas À Kempis. Abridged and Published in English by John Wesley, M.A., London. Printed at the Conference Office, North Green, Finsbury Square. G. Story, Agent. Sold By G. Whitfield, City Road. 1803. Price Bound 1s.

The book was evidently brought by Mrs. Brontë from Penzance, and given by her to her husband or left among her effects. The poor little woman had been in her grave for five or six years when it came into the hands of one of her daughters, as we learn from Charlotte's hand-writing on the fly-leaf:—

'C. Brontë's book. This book was given to me in July 1826. It is not certainly known who is the author, but it is generally supposed that Thomas à Kempis is. I saw a reward of £10,000 offered in the Leeds Mercury to any one who could find out for a certainty who is the author.'

The conjunction of the names of John Wesley, Maria Branwell, and Charlotte Brontë surely gives this little volume, 'price bound 1s.,' a singular interest!

But here I must refer to the letters which Maria Branwell wrote to her lover during the brief courtship. Mrs. Gaskell, it will be remembered, makes but one extract from this correspondence, which was handed to her by Mr. Brontë as part of the material for her memoir. Long years before, the little packet had been taken from Mr. Brontë's desk, for we find Charlotte writing to a friend on February 16th, 1850:—

'A few days since, a little incident happened which curiously touched me. Papa put into my hands a little packet of letters and papers, telling me that they were mamma's, and that I might read them. I did read them, in a frame of mind I cannot describe. The papers were yellow with time, all having been written before I was born. It was strange now to peruse, for the first time, the records of a mind whence my own sprang; and most strange, and at once sad and sweet, to find that mind of a truly fine, pure, and elevated order. They were written to papa before they were married. There is a rectitude, a refinement, a constancy, a modesty, a sense, a gentleness about them indescribable. I wish she had lived, and that I had known her.'

Yet another forty years or so and the little packet is in my possession. Handling, with a full sense of their sacredness, these letters, written more than eighty years ago by a good woman to her lover, one is tempted to hope that there is no breach of the privacy which should, even in our day, guide certain sides of life, in publishing the correspondence in its completeness. With the letters I find a little MS., which is also of pathetic interest. It is entitled 'The Advantages of Poverty in Religious Concerns,' and it is endorsed in the handwriting of Mr. Brontë, written, doubtless, many years afterwards:—

'The above was written by my dear wife, and is for insertion in one of the periodical publications. Keep it as a memorial of her.'

There is no reason to suppose that the MS. was ever published; there is no reason why any editor should have wished to publish it. It abounds in the obvious. At the same time, one notes that from both father and mother alike Charlotte Brontë and her sisters inherited some measure of the literary faculty. It is nothing to say that not one line of the father's or mother's would have been preserved had it not been for their gifted children. It is sufficient that the zest for writing was there, and that the intense passion for handling a pen, which seems to have been singularly strong in Charlotte Brontë, must have come to a great extent from a similar passion alike in father and mother. Mr. Brontë, indeed, may be counted a prolific author. He published, in all, four books, three pamphlets, and two sermons. Of his books, two were in verse and two in prose. *Cottage Poems* was published in 1811; *The Rural Minstrel* in 1812, the year of his marriage; *The Cottage in the Wood* in 1815; and *The Maid of Killarney* in 1818. After his wife's death he published no more books. Reading over these old-fashioned volumes now, one admits that they possess but little distinction. It has been pointed out, indeed, that one of the strongest lines in *Jane Eyre*—'To the finest fibre of my nature, sir.'—is culled from Mr. Brontë's verse. It is the one line of his that will live. Like his daughter Charlotte, Mr. Brontë is more interesting in his prose than in his poetry. *The Cottage in the Wood; or, the Art of Becoming Rich and Happy*, is a kind of religious novel—a spiritual *Pamela*, in which the reprobate pursuer of an innocent girl ultimately becomes converted and marries her. *The Maid of Killarney; or, Albion and Flora* is more interesting. Under the guise of a story it has something to say on many questions of importance. We know now why Charlotte never learnt to dance until she went to Brussels, and why children's games were unknown to her, for here are many mild diatribes against dancing and card-playing. The British Constitution and the British and Foreign Bible Society receive a considerable amount of criticism. But in spite of this didactic weakness there are one or two pieces of really picturesque writing, notably a description of an Irish wake, and a forcible account of the defence of a house against some Whiteboys. It is true enough that the books are merely of interest to collectors and that they live only by virtue of Patrick Brontë's remarkable children. But many a prolific writer of the day passes muster as a genius among his contemporaries upon as small a talent; and Mr. Brontë does not seem to have given himself any airs as an author. Thirty years were to elapse before there were to be any more books from this family of writers; but *Jane Eyre* owes something, we may be sure, to *The Maid of Killarney*.

Mr. Brontë, as I have said, married Maria Branwell in 1812. She was in her twenty-ninth year, and was one of five children—one son and four daughters—the father of whom, Mr. Thomas Branwell, had died in 1809. By a curious coincidence, another sister, Charlotte, was married in Penzance on the same day—the 18th of December 1812.* Before me are a bundle of samplers, worked by three of these Branwell sisters. Maria Branwell 'ended her sampler' April the 15th, 1791, and it is inscribed with the text, *Flee from sin as from a serpent, for if thou comest too near to it, it will bite thee. The teeth thereof are as the teeth of a lion to slay the souls of men.* Another sampler is by Elizabeth Branwell; another by Margaret, and another by Anne. These, some miniatures, and the book and papers to which I have referred, are all that remain to us as a memento of Mrs. Brontë, apart from the children that she bore to her husband. The miniatures, which are in the possession of Miss Branwell, of Penzance, are of Mr. and Mrs. Thomas Branwell—Charlotte Brontë's maternal grandfather and grandmother—and of Mrs. Brontë and her sister Elizabeth Branwell as children.

To return, however, to our bundle of love-letters. Comment is needless, if indeed comment or elucidation were possible at this distance of time.

---

* Mrs. Gaskell says 'Dec. 29th'; but Miss Charlotte Branwell of Penzance writes to me as follows:—'My Aunt Maria Branwell, after the death of her parents, went to Yorkshire on a visit to her relatives, where she met the Rev. Patrick Brontë. They soon became engaged to be married. Jane Fennell was previously engaged to the Rev. William Morgan. And when the time arrived for their marriage, Mr. Fennell said he should have to give his daughter and niece away, and if so, he could not marry them; so it was arranged that Mr. Morgan should marry Mr. Brontë and Maria Branwell, and afterwards Mr. Brontë should perform the same kindly office towards Mr. Morgan and Jane Fennell. So the bridegrooms married each other and the brides acted as bridesmaids to each other. My father and mother, Joseph and Charlotte Branwell, were married at Madron, which was then the parish church of Penzance, on the same day and hour. Perhaps a similar case never happened before or since: two sisters and four first cousins being united in holy matrimony at one and the same time. And they were all happy marriages. Mr. Brontë was perhaps peculiar, but I have always heard my own dear mother say that he was devotedly fond of his wife, and she of him. These marriages were solemnised on the 18th of December 1812.'

TO REV. PATRICK BRONTË, A.B., Hartshead

'Wood House Grove, *August 26th*, 1812.

'My dear Friend,—This address is sufficient to convince you that I not only permit, but approve of yours to me—I do indeed consider you as my *friend*; yet, when I consider how short a time I have had the pleasure of knowing you, I start at my own rashness, my heart fails, and did I not think that you would be disappointed and grieved at it, I believe I should be ready to spare myself the task of writing. Do not think that I am so wavering as to repent of what I have already said. No, believe me, this will never be the case, unless you give me cause for it. You need not fear that you have been mistaken in my character. If I know anything of myself, I am incapable of making an ungenerous return to the smallest degree of kindness, much less to you whose attentions and conduct have been so particularly obliging. I will frankly confess that your behaviour and what I have seen and heard of your character has excited my warmest esteem and regard, and be assured you shall never have cause to repent of any confidence you may think proper to place in me, and that it will always be my endeavour to deserve the good opinion which you have formed, although human weakness may in some instances cause me to fall short. In giving you these assurances I do not depend upon my own strength, but I look to Him who has been my unerring guide through life, and in whose continued protection and assistance I confidently trust.

'I thought on you much on Sunday, and feared you would not escape the rain. I hope you do not feel any bad effects from it? My cousin wrote you on Monday and expects this afternoon to be favoured with an answer. Your letter has caused me some foolish embarrassment, tho' in pity to my feelings they have been very sparing of their raillery.

'I will now candidly answer your questions. The *politeness of others* can never make me forget your kind attentions, neither can I *walk our accustomed rounds* without thinking on you, and, why should I be ashamed to add, wishing for your presence. If you knew what were my feelings whilst writing this you would pity me. I wish to write the truth and give you satisfaction, yet fear to go too far, and exceed the bounds of propriety. But whatever I may say or write I will *never deceive* you, or *exceed the truth*. If you think I have not placed the *utmost confidence* in you, consider my situation, and ask yourself if I have not confided in you sufficiently, perhaps too much. I am very sorry that you will not have this till after to-morrow, but it was out of my power to write sooner. I rely on your goodness to pardon everything in this which may appear either too free or too stiff; and beg that you will consider me as a warm and faithful friend.

'My uncle, aunt, and cousin unite in kind regards.

'I must now conclude with again declaring myself to be yours sincerely,

'MARIA BRANWELL.'

TO REV. PATRICK BRONTË, A.B, Hartshead

'Wood House Grove, *September 5th*, 1812.

MY DEAREST FRIEND,—I have just received your affectionate and very welcome letter, and although I shall not be able to send this until Monday, yet I cannot deny myself the pleasure of writing a few lines this evening, no longer considering it a task, but a pleasure, next to that of reading yours. I had the pleasure of hearing from Mr. Fennell, who was at Bradford on Thursday afternoon, that you had rested there all night. Had you proceeded, I am sure the walk would have been too much for you; such excessive fatigue, often repeated, must injure the strongest constitution. I am rejoiced to find that our forebodings were without cause. I had yesterday a letter from a very dear friend of mine, and had the satisfaction to learn by it that all at home are well. I feel with you the unspeakable obligations I am under to a merciful Providence—my heart swells with gratitude, and I feel an earnest desire that I may be enabled to make some suitable return to the Author of all my blessings. In general, I think I am enabled to cast my care upon Him, and then I experience a calm and peaceful serenity of mind which few things can destroy. In all my addresses to the throne of grace I never ask a blessing for myself but I beg the same for you, and considering the important station which you are called to fill, my prayers are proportionately fervent that you may be favoured with all the gifts and graces requisite for such calling. O my dear friend, let us pray much that we may live lives holy and useful to each other and all around us!

'*Monday morn.*—My cousin and I were yesterday at Coverley church, where we heard Mr. Watman preach a very excellent sermon from "learn of Me, for I am meek and lowly of heart." He displayed the character of our Saviour in a most affecting and amiable light. I scarcely ever felt more charmed with his excellencies, more grateful for his condescension, or more abased at my own unworthiness; but I lament that my heart is so little retentive of those pleasing and profitable impressions.

'I pitied you in your solitude, and felt sorry that it was not in my power to enliven it. Have you not been too hasty in informing your friends of a certain event? Why did you not leave them to guess a little longer? I shrink from the idea of its being known to every body. I do, indeed, *sometimes* think of you, but I will not say how often, lest I raise your vanity; and we sometimes talk of you and the doctor. But I believe I should seldom mention your name myself were it not now and then introduced by my cousin. I have never mentioned a word of what is past to any body. Had I thought this necessary I should have requested you to do it. But I think there is no need, as by some means or other they seem to have a pretty correct notion how matters stand betwixt us; and as their hints, etc., meet with no contradiction from me, my silence passes for confirmation. Mr. Fennell has not neglected to give me some serious and encouraging advice, and my aunt takes frequent opportunities of dropping little sentences which I may turn to some advantage. I have long had reason to know that the present state of things would give pleasure to all parties. Your ludicrous account of the scene at the Hermitage was highly diverting, we laughed heartily at it; but I fear it will not produce all that compassion in Miss Fennell's breast which you seem to wish. I will now tell you what I was thinking about and doing at the time you mention. I was then toiling up the hill with Jane and Mrs. Clapham to take our tea at Mr. Tatham's, thinking on the evening when I first took the same walk with you, and on the change which had taken place in my circumstances and views since then—not wholly without a wish that I had your arm to assist me, and your conversation to shorten the walk. Indeed, all our walks have now an insipidity in them which I never thought they would have possessed. When I work, if I wish to get *forward* I may be glad that you are at a distance. Jane begs me to assure you of her kind regards. Mr. Morgan is expected to be here this evening. I must assume a bold and steady countenance to meet his attacks!

'I have now written a pretty long letter without reserve or caution, and if all the sentiments of my heart are not laid open to you, believe me it is not because I wish them to be concealed, for I hope there is nothing there that would give you pain or displeasure. My most sincere and earnest wishes are for your happiness and welfare, for this includes my own. Pray much for me that I may be made a blessing and not a hindrance to you. Let me not interrupt your studies nor intrude on that time which ought to be dedicated to better purposes. Forgive my freedom, my dearest friend, and rest assured that you are and ever will be dear to

MARIA BRANWELL.
'Write very soon.'

TO REV. PATRICK BRONTË, A.B., Hartshead

'Wood House Grove, *September* 11*th*, 1812.

'MY DEAREST FRIEND,—Having spent the day yesterday at Miry Shay, a place near Bradford, I had not got your letter till my return in the evening, and consequently have only a short time this morning to write if I send it by this post. You surely do not think you *trouble* me by writing? No, I think I may venture to say if such were your opinion you would *trouble* me no more. Be assured, your letters are and I hope always will be received with extreme pleasure and read with delight. May our Gracious Father mercifully grant the fulfilment of your prayers! Whilst we depend entirely on Him for happiness, and receive each other and all our blessings as from His hands, what can harm us or make us miserable? Nothing temporal or spiritual.

'Jane had a note from Mr. Morgan last evening, and she desires me to tell you that the Methodists' service in church hours is to commence next Sunday week. You may expect frowns and hard words from her when you make your appearance here again, for, if you recollect, she gave you a note to carry to the Doctor, and he has never received it. What have you done with it? If you can give a good account of it you may come to see us as soon as you please and be sure of a hearty welcome from all parties. Next Wednesday we have some thoughts, if the weather be fine, of going to Kirkstall Abbey once more, and I suppose your presence will not make the walk less agreeable to any of us.

'The old man is come and waits for my letter. In expectation of seeing you on Monday or Tuesday next,—I remain, yours faithfully and affectionately,

'M. B.'

TO REV. PATRICK BRONTË, A.B., Hartshead

'Wood House Grove, *September* 18*th*, 1812.

'How readily do I comply with my dear Mr. B's request! You see, you have only to express your wishes and as far as my power extends I hesitate not to fulfil them. My heart tells me that it will always be my pride and pleasure to contribute to your happiness, nor do I fear that this will ever be inconsistent with my duty as a Christian. My esteem for you and my confidence in you is so great, that I firmly believe you will never exact anything from me which I could not conscientiously perform. I shall in future look to you for assistance and instruction whenever I may need them, and hope you will never withhold from me any advice or caution you may see necessary.

['For some years I have been perfectly my own mistress, subject to no control whatever—so far from it, that my sisters who are many years older than myself, and even my dear mother, used to consult me in every case of importance, and scarcely ever doubted the propriety of my opinions and actions. Perhaps you will be ready to accuse me of vanity in mentioning this, but you must consider that I do not *boast* of it, I have many times felt it a disadvantage; and although, I thank God, it never led me into error, yet in circumstances of perplexity and doubt, I have deeply felt the want of a guide and instructor.]*

'At such times I have seen and felt the necessity of supernatural aid, and by fervent applications to a throne of grace I have experienced that my heavenly Father is able and willing to supply the place of every earthly friend. I shall now no longer feel this want, this sense of helpless weakness, for I believe a kind Providence has intended that I shall find in you every earthly friend united; nor do I fear to trust myself under your protection, or shrink from your control. It is pleasant to be subject to those we love, especially when they never exert their authority but for the good of the subject. How few would write in this way! But I do not fear that *you* will make a bad use of it. You tell me to write my thoughts, and thus as they occur I freely let my pen run away with them.

'*Sat. morn.*—I do not know whether you dare show your face here again or not after the blunder you have committed. When we got to the house on Thursday evening, even before we were within the doors, we found that Mr. and Mrs. Bedford had been there, and that they had requested you to mention their intention of coming—a single hint of which you never gave! Poor I too came in for a share in the hard words which were bestowed upon you, for they all agreed that I was the cause of it. Mr. Fennell said you were certainly *mazed*, and talked of sending you to York, etc. And even I begin to think that *this*, together with the *note*, bears some marks of *insanity*! However, I shall suspend my judgment until I hear what excuse you can make for yourself, I suppose you will be quite ready to make one of some kind or another.

'Yesterday I performed a difficult and yet a pleasing task in writing to my sisters. I thought I never should accomplish the end for which the letter was designed; but after a good deal of perambulation I gave them to understand the nature of my engagement with you, with the motives and inducements

---

* The passage in brackets is quoted by Mrs. Gaskell.

which led me to form such an engagement, and that in consequence of it I should not see them again so soon as I had intended. I concluded by expressing a hope that they would not be less pleased with the information than were my friends here. I think they will not suspect me to have made a wrong step, their partiality for me is so great. And their affection for me will lead them to rejoice in my welfare, even though it should diminish somewhat of their own. I shall think the time tedious till I hear from you, and must beg you will write as soon as possible. Pardon me, my dear friend, if I again caution you against giving way to a weakness of which I have heard you complain. When you find your heart oppressed and your thoughts too much engrossed by one subject, let prayer be your refuge—this you no doubt know by experience to be a sure remedy, and a relief from every care and error. Oh, that we had more of the spirit of prayer! I feel that I need it much.

'Breakfast-time is near, I must bid you farewell for the time, but rest assured you will always share in the prayers and heart of your own

MARIA.

'Mr. Fennell has crossed my letter to my sisters. With his usual goodness he has supplied my *deficiencies*, and spoken of me in terms of commendation of which I wish I were more worthy. Your character he has likewise displayed in the most favourable light; and I am sure they will not fail to love and esteem you though unknown.

'All here unite in kind regards. Adieu.'

TO REV. PATRICK BRONTË A.B., Hartshead

'Wood House Grove, *September* 23rd, 1812.

'MY DEAREST FRIEND,—Accept of my warmest thanks for your kind affectionate letter, in which you have rated mine so highly that I really blush to read my own praises. Pray that God would enable me to deserve all the kindness you manifest towards me, and to act consistently with the good opinion you entertain of me—then I shall indeed be a helpmeet for you, and to be this shall at all times be the care and study of my future life. We have had to-day a large party of the Bradford folks—the Rands, Fawcets, Dobsons, etc. My thoughts often strayed from the company, and I would have gladly left them to follow my present employment. To write to and receive letters from my friends were always among my chief enjoyments, but none ever gave me so much pleasure as those which I receive from and write to my newly adopted friend. I am by no means sorry you have given up all thought of the house you mentioned. With my cousin's help I have made known your plans to my uncle and aunt. Mr. Fennell immediately coincided with that which respects your present abode, and observed that it had occurred to him before, but that he had not had an opportunity of mentioning it to you. My aunt did not fall in with it so readily, but her objections did not appear to me to be very weighty. For my own part, I feel all the force of your arguments in favour of it, and the objections are so trifling that they can scarcely be called objections. My cousin is of the same opinion. Indeed, you have such a method of considering and digesting a plan before you make it known to your friends, that you run very little risque of incurring their disapprobations, or of having your schemes frustrated. I greatly admire your talents this way—may they never be perverted by being used in a bad cause! And whilst they are exerted for good purposes, may they prove irresistible! If I may judge from your letter, this middle scheme is what would please you best, so that if there should arise no new objection to it, perhaps it will prove the best you can adopt. However, there is yet sufficient time to consider it further. I trust in this and every other circumstance you will be guided by the wisdom that cometh from above—a portion of which I doubt not has guided you hitherto. A belief of this, added to the complete satisfaction with which I read your reasonings on the subject, made me a ready convert to your opinions. I hope nothing will occur to induce you to change your intention of spending the next week at Bradford. Depend on it you shall have letter for letter; but may we not hope to see you here during that time, surely you will not think the way more tedious than usual? I have not heard any particulars respecting the church since you were at Bradford. Mr. Rawson is now there, but Mr. Hardy and his brother are absent, and I understand nothing decisive can be accomplished without them. Jane expects to hear something more to-morrow. Perhaps ere this reaches you, you will have received some intelligence respecting it from Mr. Morgan. If you have no other apology to make for your blunders than that which you have given me, you must not expect to be excused, for I have not mentioned it to any one, so that however it may clear your character in my opinion it is not likely to influence any other person. Little, very little, will induce me to cover your faults with a veil of charity. I already feel a kind of participation in all that concerns you. All praises and censures bestowed on you must equally affect me. Your joys and sorrows must be mine. Thus shall the one be increased and the other diminished. While this is the case we shall, I hope, always find "life's cares" to be "comforts." And may we feel every trial and distress, for such must be our lot at times, bind us nearer to God and to each other! My heart earnestly joins in your comprehensive prayers. I trust they will unitedly ascend to a throne of grace, and through the Redeemer's merits procure for us peace and happiness here and a life of eternal felicity hereafter. Oh, what sacred pleasure there is in the idea of spending an eternity together in perfect and uninterrupted bliss! This should encourage us to the utmost exertion and fortitude. But whilst I write, my own words condemn me—I am ashamed of my own indolence and backwardness to duty. May I be more careful, watchful, and active than I have ever yet been!

'My uncle, aunt, and Jane request me to send their kind regards, and they will be happy to see you any time next week whenever you can conveniently come down from Bradford. Let me hear from you soon—I shall expect a letter on Monday. Farewell, my dearest friend. That you may be happy in yourself and very useful to all around you is the daily earnest prayer of yours truly,

'Maria Branwell.'

TO REV. PATRICK BRONTË, A.B., Hartshead

'Wood House Grove, *October 3rd*, 1812.

'How could my dear friend so cruelly disappoint me? Had he known how much I had set my heart on having a letter this afternoon, and how greatly I felt the disappointment when the bag arrived and I found there was nothing for me, I am sure he would not have permitted a little matter to hinder him. But whatever was the reason of your not writing, I cannot believe it to have been neglect or unkindness, therefore I do not in the least blame you, I only beg that in future you will judge of my feelings by your own, and if possible never let me expect a letter without receiving one. You know in my last which I sent you at Bradford I said it would not be in my power to write the next day, but begged I might be favoured with hearing from you on Saturday, and you will not wonder that I hoped you would have complied with this request. It has just occurred to my mind that it is possible this note was not received; if so, you have felt disappointed likewise; but I think this is not very probable, as the old man is particularly careful, and I never heard of his losing anything committed to his care. The note which I allude to was written on Thursday morning, and you should have received it before you left Bradford. I forget what its contents were, but I know it was written in haste and concluded abruptly. Mr. Fennell talks of visiting Mr. Morgan tomorrow. I cannot lose the opportunity of sending this to the office by him as you will then have it a day sooner, and if you have been daily expecting to hear from me, twenty-four hours are of some importance. I really am concerned to find that this, what many would deem trifling incident, has so much disturbed my mind. I fear I should not have slept in peace to-night if I had been deprived of this opportunity of relieving my mind by scribbling to you, and now I lament that you cannot possibly receive this till Monday. May I hope that there is now some intelligence on the way to me? or must my patience be tried till I see you on Wednesday? But what nonsense am I writing? Surely after this you can have no doubt that you possess all my heart. Two months ago I could not possibly have believed that you would ever engross so much of my thoughts and affections, and far less could I have thought that I should be so forward as to tell you so. I believe I must forbid you to come here again unless you can assure me that you will not steal any more of my regard. Enough of this; I must bring my pen to order, for if I were to suffer myself to revise what I have written I should be tempted to throw it in the fire, but I have determined that you shall see my whole heart. I have not yet informed you that I received your serio-comic note on Thursday afternoon, for which accept my thanks.

'My cousin desires me to say that she expects a long poem on her birthday, when she attains the important age of twenty-one. Mr. Fennell joins with us in requesting that you will not fail to be here on Wednesday, as it is decided that on Thursday we are to go to the Abbey if the weather, etc., permits.

'*Sunday morning.*—I am not sure if I do right in adding a few lines to-day, but knowing that it will give you pleasure I wish to finish that you may have it to-morrow. I will just say that if my feeble prayers can aught avail, you will find your labours this day both pleasant and profitable, as they concern your own soul and the souls of those to whom you preach. I trust in your hours of retirement you will not forget to pray for me. I assure you I need every assistance to help me forward; I feel that my heart is more ready to attach itself to earth than heaven. I sometimes think there never was a mind so dull and inactive as mine is with regard to spiritual things.

'I must not forget to thank you for the pamphlets and tracts which you sent us from Bradford. I hope we shall make good use of them. I must now take my leave. I believe I need scarcely assure you that I am yours truly and very affectionately,

'Maria Branwell.'

TO REV. PATRICK BRONTË, A.B., Hartshead

'Wood House Grove, *October* 21*st* 1812.

'With the sincerest pleasure do I retire from company to converse with him whom I love beyond all others. Could my beloved friend see my heart he would then be convinced that the affection I bear him is not at all inferior to that which he feels for me—indeed I sometimes think that in truth and constancy it excels. But do not think from this that I entertain any suspicions of your sincerity—no, I firmly believe you to be sincere and generous, and doubt not in the least that you feel all you express. In return, I entreat that you will do me the justice to believe that you have not only a *very large portion* of my *affection* and *esteem*, but *all* that I am capable of feeling, and from henceforth measure my feelings by your own. Unless my love for you were very great how could I so contentedly give up my home and all my friends—a home I loved so much that I have often thought nothing could bribe me to renounce it for any great length of time together, and friends with whom I have been so long accustomed to share all the vicissitudes of joy and sorrow? Yet these have lost their weight, and though I cannot always think of them without a sigh, yet the anticipation of sharing with you all the pleasures and pains, the cares and anxieties of life, of contributing to your comfort and becoming the companion of your pilgrimage, is more delightful to me than any other prospect which this world can possibly present. I expected to have heard from you on Saturday last, and can scarcely refrain from thinking you unkind to keep me in suspense two whole days longer than was necessary, but it is well that my patience should be sometimes tried, or I might entirely lose it, and this would be a loss indeed! Lately I have experienced a considerable increase of hopes and fears, which tend to destroy the calm uniformity of my life. These are not unwelcome, as they enable me to discover more of the evils and errors of my heart, and discovering them I hope through grace to be enabled to correct and amend them. I am sorry to say that my cousin has had a very serious cold, but to-day I think she is better; her cough seems less, and I hope we shall be able to come to Bradford on Saturday afternoon, where we intend to stop till Tuesday. You may be sure we shall not soon think of taking such another journey as the last. I look forward with pleasure to Monday, when I hope to meet with you, for as we are no *longer twain* separation is painful, and to meet must ever be attended with joy.

'*Thursday morning.*—I intended to have finished this before breakfast, but unfortunately slept an hour too long. I am every moment in expectation of the old man's arrival. I hope my cousin is still better to-day; she requests me to say that she is much obliged to you for your kind inquiries and the concern you express for her recovery. I take all possible care of her, but yesterday she was naughty enough to venture into the yard without her bonnet! As you do not say anything of going to Leeds I conclude you have not been. We shall most probably hear from the Dr. this afternoon. I am much pleased to hear of his success at Bierly! O that you may both be zealous and successful in your efforts for the salvation of souls, and may your own lives be holy, and your hearts greatly blessed while you are engaged in administering to the good of others! I should have been very glad to have had it in my power to lessen your fatigue and cheer your spirits by my exertions on Monday last. I will hope that this pleasure is still reserved for me. In general, I feel a calm confidence in the providential care and continued mercy of God, and when I consider his past deliverances and past favours I am led to wonder and adore. A sense of my small returns of love and gratitude to him often abases me and makes me think I am little better than those who profess no religion. Pray for me, my dear friend, and rest assured that you possess a very very large portion of the prayers, thoughts, and heart of yours truly,

'M. Branwell.

'Mr. Fennell requests Mr. Bedford to call on the man who has had orders to make blankets for the Grove and desire him to send them as soon as possible. Mr. Fennell will be greatly obliged to Mr. Bedford if he will take this trouble.'

TO REV. PATRICK BRONTË, A.B., Hartshcad

'Wood House Grove, *November* 18*th*, 1812.

'My dear saucy Pat,—Now don't you think you deserve this epithet far more than I do that which you have given me? I really know not what to make of the beginning of your last; the winds, waves, and rocks almost stunned me. I thought you were giving me the account of some terrible dream, or that you had had a presentiment of the fate of my poor box, having no idea that your lively imagination could make so much of the slight reproof conveyed in my last. What will you say when you get a *real, downright scolding*? Since you show such a readiness to atone for your offences after receiving a mild rebuke, I am inclined to hope you will seldom deserve a severe one. I accept with pleasure your atonement, and send you a free and full forgiveness. But I cannot allow that your affection is more deeply rooted than mine. However, we will dispute no more about this, but rather embrace every opportunity to prove its sincerity and strength by acting in every respect as friends and fellow-pilgrims travelling the same road, actuated by the same motives, and having in view the same end. I think if our lives are spared twenty years hence I shall then pray for you with the same, if not greater, fervour and delight that I do now. I am pleased that you are so fully convinced of my candour, for to know that you suspected me of a deficiency in this virtue would grieve and mortify me beyond expression. I do not derive any merit from the possession of it, for in me it is constitutional. Yet I think where it is possessed it will rarely exist alone, and where it is wanted there is reason to doubt the existence of almost every other virtue. As to the other qualities which your partiality attributes to me, although I rejoice to know that I stand so high in your good opinion, yet I blush to think in how small a degree I possess them. But it shall be the pleasing study of my future life to gain such an increase of grace and wisdom as shall enable me to act up to your highest expectations and prove to you a helpmeet. I firmly believe the Almighty has set us apart for each other; may we, by earnest, frequent prayer, and every possible exertion, endeavour to fulfil His will in all things! I do not, cannot, doubt your love, and here I freely declare I love you above all the world besides. I feel very, very grateful to the great Author of all our mercies for His unspeakable love and condescension towards us, and desire "to show forth my gratitude not only with my lips, but by my life and conversation." I indulge a hope that our mutual prayers will be answered, and that our intimacy will tend much to promote our temporal and eternal interest.

['I suppose you never expected to be much the richer for me, but I am sorry to inform you that I am still poorer than I thought myself. I mentioned having sent for my books, clothes, etc. On Saturday evening about the time you were writing the description of your imaginary shipwreck, I was reading and feeling the effects of a real one, having then received a letter from my sister giving me an account of the vessel in which she had sent my box being stranded on the coast of Devonshire, in consequence of which the box was dashed to pieces with the violence of the sea, and all my little property, with the exception of a very few articles, swallowed up in the mighty deep. If this should not prove the prelude to something worse, I shall think little of it, as it is the first disastrous circumstance which has occurred since I left my home],* and having been so highly favoured it would be highly ungrateful in

---

* The passage in brackets is quoted, not quite accurately, by Mrs. Gaskell.

me were I to suffer this to dwell much on my mind.

'Mr. Morgan was here yesterday, indeed he only left this morning. He mentioned having written to invite you to Bierly on Sunday next, and if you complied with his request it is likely that we shall see you both here on Sunday evening. As we intend going to Leeds next week, we should be happy if you would accompany us on Monday or Tuesday. I mention this by desire of Miss Fennell, who begs to be remembered affectionately to you. Notwithstanding Mr. Fennell's complaints and threats, I doubt not but he will give you a cordial reception whenever you think fit to make your appearance at the Grove. Which you may likewise be assured of receiving from your ever truly affectionate,

MARIA.

'Both the doctor and his lady very much wish to know what kind of address we make use of in our letters to each other. I think they would scarcely hit on *this*!!'

TO REV. PATRICK BRONTË, A.B., Hartshead

'Wood House Grove, *December* 5*th*, 1812.

'MY DEAREST FRIEND,—So you *thought* that *perhaps* I *might* expect to hear from you. As the case was so doubtful, and you were in such great haste, you might as well have deferred writing a few days longer, for you seem to suppose it is a matter of perfect indifference to me whether I hear from you or not. I believe I once requested you to judge of my feelings by your own—am I to think that *you* are thus indifferent? I feel very unwilling to entertain such an opinion, and am grieved that you should suspect me of such a cold, heartless, attachment. But I am too serious on the subject; I only meant to rally you a little on the beginning of your last, and to tell you that I fancied there was a coolness in it which none of your former letters had contained. If this fancy was groundless, forgive me for having indulged it, and let it serve to convince you of the sincerity and warmth of my affection. Real love is ever apt to suspect that it meets not with an equal return; you must not wonder then that my fears are sometimes excited. My pride cannot bear the idea of a diminution of your attachment, or to think that it is stronger on my side than on yours. But I must not permit my pen so fully to disclose the feelings of my heart, nor will I tell you whether I am pleased or not at the thought of seeing you on the appointed day.

'Miss Fennell desires her kind regards, and, with her father, is extremely obliged to you for the trouble you have taken about the carpet, and has no doubt but it will give full satisfaction. They think there will be no occasion for the green cloth.

'We intend to set about making the cakes here next week, but as the fifteen or twenty persons whom you mention live probably somewhere in your neighbourhood, I think it will be most convenient for Mrs. B. to make a small one for the purpose of distributing there, which will save us the difficulty of sending so far.

'You may depend on my learning my lessons as rapidly as they are given me. I am already tolerably perfect in the A B C, etc. I am much obliged to you for the pretty little hymn which I have already got by heart, but cannot promise to sing it scientifically, though I will endeavour to gain a little more assurance.

'Since I began this Jane put into my hands Lord Lyttelton's *Advice to a Lady*. When I read those lines, "Be never cool reserve with passion joined, with caution choose, but then be fondly kind, etc." my heart smote me for having in some cases used too much reserve towards you. Do you think you have any cause to complain of me? If you do, let me know it. For were it in my power to prevent it, I would in no instance occasion you the least pain or uneasiness. I am certain no one ever loved you with an affection more pure, constant, tender, and ardent than that which I feel. Surely this is not saying too much; it is the truth, and I trust you are worthy to know it. I long to improve in every religious and moral quality, that I may be a help, and if possible an ornament to you. Oh let us pray much for wisdom and grace to fill our appointed stations with propriety, that we may enjoy satisfaction in our own souls, edify others, and bring glory to the name of Him who has so wonderfully preserved, blessed, and brought us together.

'If there is anything in the commencement of this which looks like pettishness, forgive it; my mind is now completely divested of every feeling of the kind, although I own I am sometimes too apt to be overcome by this disposition.

'Let me have the pleasure of hearing from you again as soon as convenient. This writing is uncommonly bad, but I too am in haste.

'Adieu, my dearest.—I am your affectionate and sincere

'Maria.'

Mr. Brontë was at Hartshead, where he married, for five years, and there his two eldest children, Maria and Elizabeth, were born. He then moved to Thornton, near Bradford, where Charlotte was born on the 21st of April 1816, Branwell in 1817, Emily in 1818, and Anne in 1819. In 1820 the family removed to the parsonage of Haworth, and in 1821 the poor mother was dead. A year or two later Miss Elizabeth Branwell came from Penzance to act as a mother to her orphaned nephew and nieces. There is no reason to accept the theory that Miss Branwell was quite as formidable or offensive a personage as the Mrs. Read in *Jane Eyre*. That she was a somewhat rigid and not over demonstrative woman, we may take for granted. The one letter to her of any importance that I have seen—it is printed in Mrs. Gaskell's life—was the attempt of Charlotte to obtain her co-operation in the projected visit to a Brussels school. Miss Branwell provided the money readily enough it would seem, and one cannot doubt that in her later years she was on the best of terms with her nieces. There may have been too much discipline in childhood, but discipline which would now be considered too severe was common enough at the beginning of the century. The children, we may be sure, were left abundantly alone. The writing they accomplished in their early years would sufficiently demonstrate that. Miss Branwell died in 1842; and from her will, which I give elsewhere, it will be seen that she behaved very justly to her three nieces.

The reception by Mr. Brontë of his children's literary successes has been very pleasantly recorded by Charlotte. He was proud of his daughters, and delighted with their fame. He seems to have had no small share of their affection. Charlotte loved and esteemed him. There are hundreds of her letters, in many of which are severe and indeed unprintable things about this or that individual; but of her father these letters contain not one single harsh word. She wrote to him regularly when absent. Not only did he secure the affection of his daughter, but the people most intimately associated with him next to his own children gave him a lifelong affection and regard. Martha Brown, the servant who lived with him until his death, always insisted that her old master had been grievously wronged, and that a kinder, more generous, and in every way more worthy man had never lived. Nancy Garrs, another servant, always spoke of Mr. Brontë as 'the kindest man who ever drew breath,' and as a good and affectionate father. Forty years have gone by since Charlotte Brontë died; and thirty-six years have flown since Mr. Nicholls left the deathbed of his wife's father; but through all that period he has retained the most kindly memories of one with whom his life was intimately associated for sixteen years, with whom at one crisis of his life, as we shall see, he had a serious difference, but whom he ever believed to have been an entirely honourable and upright man.

A lady visitor to Haworth in December 1860 did not, it is true, carry away quite so friendly an impression. 'I have been to see old Mr. Brontë,' she writes, 'and have spent about an hour with him. He is completely confined to his bed, but talks hopefully of leaving it again when the summer comes round. I am afraid that it will not be leaving it as he plans, poor old man! He is touchingly softened by illness; but still talks in his pompous way, and mingles moral remarks and somewhat stale sentiments with his conversation on ordinary subjects.' This is severe, but after all it was a literary woman who wrote it. On the whole we may safely assume, with the evidence before us, that Mr. Brontë was a thoroughly upright and honourable man who came manfully through a somewhat severe life battle. That is how his daughters thought of him, and we cannot do better than think with them.'

Mr. Brontë died on June 7, 1861, and his funeral in Haworth Church is described in the *Bradford Review* of the following week:—

---

* The following letter indicates Mr. Brontë's independence of spirit. It was written after Charlotte's death:

'Haworth, nr. Keighley, January 16th, 1858.

'Sir,—Your letter which I have received this morning gives both to Mr. Nicholls and me great uneasiness. It would seem that application has been made to the Duke of Devonshire for money to aid the subscription in reference to the expense of apparatus for heating our church and schools. This has been done without our knowledge, and most assuredly, had we known it, would have met with our strongest opposition. We have no claim on the Duke. His Grace honour'd us with a visit, in token of his respect for the memory of the dead, and his liberality and munificence are well and widely known; and the mercenary, taking an unfair advantage of these circumstances, have taken a step which both Mr. Nicholls and I utterly regret and condemn. In answer to your query, I may state that the whole expense for both the schools and church is about one hundred pounds; and that after what has been and may be subscribed, there may fifty pounds remain as a debt. But this may, and ought, to be raised by the inhabitants, in the next year after the depression of trade shall, it is hoped, have passed away. I have written to His Grace on the subject—I remain, sir, your obedient servant,

'P. Brontë.

'Sir Joseph Paxton, Bart.,
'Hardwick Hall, 'Chesterfield.'

'Great numbers of people had collected in the churchyard, and a few minutes before noon the corpse was brought out through the eastern gate of the garden leading into the churchyard. The Rev. Dr. Burnet, Vicar of Bradford, read the funeral service, and led the way into the church, and the following clergymen were the bearers of the coffin: The Rev. Dr. Cartman of Skipton; Rev. Mr. Sowden of Hebden Bridge; the Incumbents of Cullingworth, Oakworth, Morton, Oxenhope, and St. John's Ingrow. The chief mourners were the Rev. Arthur Bell Nicholls, son-in-law of the deceased; Martha Brown, the housekeeper; and her sister; Mrs. Brown, and Mrs. Wainwright. There were several gentlemen followed the corpse whom we did not know. All the shops in Haworth were closed, and the people filled every pew, and the aisles in the church, and many shed tears during the impressive reading of the service for the burial of the dead, by the vicar. The body of Mr. Brontë was laid within the altar rails, by the side of his daughter Charlotte. He is the last that can be interred inside of Haworth Church. On the coffin was this inscription: "Patrick Brontë, died June 7th, 1861, aged 84 years."'

His will, which was proved at Wakefield, left the bulk of his property, as was natural, to the son-in-law who had faithfully served and tended him for the six years which succeeded Charlotte Brontë's death.

Extracted from the Principal Registry of the Probate Divorce and Admiralty Division of the High Court of Justice.

Being of sound mind and judgment, in the name of God the Father, Son, and Holy Ghost, I, Patrick Brontë, B.A., *Incumbent of Haworth, in the Parish of Bradford and county of York, make this my last Will and Testament: I leave forty pounds to be equally divided amongst all my brothers and sisters to whom I gave considerable sums in times past; And I direct the same sum of forty pounds to be sent for distribution to Mr. Hugh Brontë, Ballinasceaugh, near Loughbrickland, Ireland; I leave thirty pounds to my servant, Martha Brown, as a token of regard for long and faithful services to me and my children; To my beloved and esteemed son-in-law, the Rev. Arthur Bell Nicholls, B.A., I leave and bequeath the residue of my personal estate of every description which I shall be possessed of at my death for his own absolute benefit; And I make him my sole executor; And I revoke all former and other Wills, in witness whereof I, the said* Patrick Brontë, *have to this my last Will, contained in this sheet of paper, set my hand this twentieth day of June, one thousand eight hundred and fifty-five.*

PATRICK BRONTË.—*Signed and acknowledged by the said* PATRICK BRONTË *as his Will in the presence of us present at the same time, and who in his presence and in the presence of each other have hereunto subscribed our names as witnesses*: JOSEPH REDMAN, ELIZA BROWN.

The Irish relatives are not forgotten, and indeed this will gives the most direct evidence of the fact that for the sixty years that he had been absent from his native land he had always kept his own country, or at least his relatives in County Down, sufficiently in mind.

HAWORTH: NOVEMBER 1904

By Virginia Woolf

Haworth was the home of the Brontë family. Virginia Woolf's account of a visit to Haworth was the first of her writings to be accepted for publication (and the second to appear in print.) Woolf's article was first published in *The Guardian*, unsigned, on 21st December, 1904.

I do not know whether pilgrimages to the shrines of famous men ought not to be condemned as sentimental journeys. It is better to read Carlyle in your own study chair than to visit the sound-proof room and pore over the manuscripts at Chelsea. I should be inclined to set up an examination on Frederick the Great in place of an entrance fee; only, in that case, the house would soon have to be shut up. The curiosity is only legitimate when the house of a great writer or the country in which it is set adds something to our understanding of his books. This justification you have for a pilgrimage to the home and country of Charlotte Brontë and her sisters.

The *Life*, by Mrs Gaskell, gives you the impression that Haworth and the Brontës are somehow inextricably mixed. Haworth expresses the Brontës; the Brontës express Haworth; they fit like a snail to its shell. How far surroundings radically affect people's minds, it is not for me to ask: superficially, the influence is great, but it is worth asking if the famous parsonage had been placed in a London slum, the dens of Whitechapel would not have had the same result as the lonely Yorkshire moors. However, I am taking away my only excuse for visiting Haworth. Unreasonable or not, one of the chief points of a recent visit to Yorkshire was that an expedition to Haworth could be accomplished. The necessary arrangements were made, and we determined to take advantage of the first day for our expedition. A real northern snowstorm had been doing the honours of the moors. It was rash to wait fine weather, and it was also cowardly. I understand that the sun very seldom shone on the Brontë family, and if we chose a really fine day we should have to make allowance for the fact that fifty years ago there were few fine days at Haworth, and that we were, therefore, for sake of comfort, rubbing out half the shadows on the picture. However, it would be interesting to see what impression Haworth could make upon the brilliant weather of Settle. We certainly passed through a very cheerful land, which might be likened to a vast wedding cake, of which the icing was slightly undulating; the earth was bridal in its virgin snow, which helped to suggest the comparison.

Keighley—pronounced Keethly—is often mentioned in the *Life*; it was the big town four miles from Haworth in which Charlotte walked to make her more important purchases—her wedding gown, perhaps, and the thin little cloth boots which we examined under glass in the Brontë Museum. It is a big manufacturing town, hard and stony, and clattering with business, in the way of these Northern towns. They make small provision for the sentimental traveller, and our only occupation was to picture the slight figure of Charlotte trotting along the streets in her thin mantle, hustled into the gutter by more burly passers-by. It was the Keighley of her day, and that was some comfort. Our excitement as we neared Haworth had in it an element of suspense that was really painful, as though we were to meet some long-separated friend, who might have changed in the interval—so clear an image of Haworth had we from print and picture. At a certain point we entered the valley, up both sides of which the village climbs, and right on the hill-top, looking down over its parish, we saw the famous oblong tower of the church. This marked the shrine at which we were to do homage.

It may have been the effect of a sympathetic imagination, but I think that there were good reasons why Haworth did certainly strike one not exactly as gloomy, but, what is worse for artistic purposes, as dingy and commonplace. The houses, built of yellow-brown stone, date from the early nineteenth century. They climb the moor step by step in little detached strips, some distance apart, so that the town instead of making one compact blot on the landscape has contrived to get a whole stretch into its clutches. There is a long line of houses up the moor-side, which clusters round the church and parsonage with a little clump of trees. At the top the interest for a Brontë lover becomes suddenly intense. The church, the parsonage, the Brontë Museum, the school where Charlotte taught, and the Bull Inn where Branwell drank are all within a stone's throw of each other. The museum is certainly rather a pallid and inanimate collection of objects. An effort ought to be made to keep things out of these mausoleums, but the choice often lies between them and destruction, so that we must be grateful for the care which has preserved much that is, under any circumstances, of deep interest. Here are many autograph letters, pencil drawings, and other documents. But the most touching case—so touching that one hardly feels reverent in one's gaze—is that which contains the little personal relics of the dead woman. The natural fate of such things is to die before the body that wore them, and because these, trifling and transient though they are, have survived, Charlotte Brontë the woman comes to life, and one forgets the chiefly memorable fact that she was a great writer. Her shoes and her thin muslin dress have outlived her. One other object gives a thrill; the little oak stool which Emily carried with her on her solitary moorland tramps, and on which she sat, if not to write, as they say, to think what was probably better than her writing.

The church, of course, save part of the tower, is renewed since Brontë days; but that remarkable churchyard remains. The old edition of the *Life* had on its title-page a little print which struck the keynote of the book; it seemed to be all graves—gravestones stood ranked all round; you walked on a pavement lettered with dead names; the graves had solemnly invaded the garden of the parsonage itself, which was as a little oasis of life in the midst of the dead. This is no exaggeration of the artist's, as we found: the stones seem to start out of the ground at you in tall, upright lines, like and army of silent soldiers. there is no hand's breadth untenanted; indeed, the economy of space is somewhat irreverent. In old days a flagged path, which suggested the slabs of graves, led from the front door of the parsonage to the churchyard without interruption of wall or hedge; the garden was practically the graveyard too; the successors of the Brontës, however, wishing a little space between life and death, planted a hedge and several tall trees, which now cut off the parsonage garden completely. The house itself is precisely the same as it was in Charlotte's day, save that one new wing has been added. It is easy to shut the eye to this, and then you have the square, boxlike parsonage, built of the ugly yellow-brown stone which they quarry from the moors behind, precisely as it was when Charlotte lived and died there. Inside, of course, the changes are many, though not such as to obscure the original shape of the rooms. There is nothing remarkable in a mid-Victorian parsonage, though tenanted by genius, and the only room which awakens curiosity is the kitchen, now used as an ante-room, in which the girls tramped as they conceived their work. One other spot has a certain grim interest—the oblong recess beside the staircase into which Emily drove her bulldog during the famous fight, and pinned him while she pommelled him. It is otherwise a little sparse parsonage, much like others of its kind. It was due to the courtesy of the present incumbent that we were allowed to inspect it; in his place I should often feel inclined to exorcise the three famous ghosts.

One thing only remained: the church in which Charlotte worshipped, was married, and lies buried. The circumference of her life was very narrow. Here, though much is altered, a few things remain to tell of her. The slab which bears the names of the succession of children and of their parents—their births and deaths—strikes the eye first. Name follows name; at very short intervals they died—Maria the mother, Maria the daughter, Elizabeth, Branwell, Emily, Anne, Charlotte, and lastly the old father, who outlived them all. Emily was only thirty years old, and Charlotte but nine years older. 'The sting of death is sin, and the strength of sin is the law, but thanks be to God which giveth us the victory through our Lord Jesus Christ.' That is the inscription which has been placed beneath their names, and with reason; for however harsh the struggle, Emily, and Charlotte above all, fought to victory.

COTTAGE POEMS

EPISTLE TO THE REV. J--- B---

WHILST JOURNEYING FOR THE RECOVERY OF HIS HEALTH

When warm'd with zeal, my rustic Muse
Feels fluttering fain to tell her news,
And paint her simple, lowly views
    With all her art,
And, though in genius but obtuse,
    May touch the heart.

Of palaces and courts of kings
She thinks but little, never sings,
But wildly strikes her uncouth strings
    In some pool cot,
Spreads o'er the poor hen fostering wings,
    And soothes their lot.

Well pleased is she to see them smile,
And uses every honest wile
To mend then hearts, their cares beguile,
    With rhyming story,
And lend them to then God the while,
    And endless glory.

Perchance, my poor neglected Muse
Unfit to harass or amuse,
Escaping praise and loud abuse,
    Unheard, unknown,
May feed the moths and wasting dews,
    As some have done.

Her aims are good, howe'er they end—
Here comes a foe, and there a friend,
These point the dart and those defend,
    Whilst some deride her;
But God will sweetest comforts blend,
    Whate'er betide her.

Thus heaven-supported, forth she goes
Midst flatterers, critics, friends, and foes;
Secure, since He who all things knows
    Approves her aim,
And kindly fans, or fostering blows
    Her sinking flame.

Hence, when she shows her honest face,
And tells her tale with awkward grace,
Importunate to gain a place
    Amongst your friends,
To ruthless critics leave her case,
    And hail her ends.

To all my heart is kind and true,
But glows with ardent love for you;
Though absent, still you rise in view,
    And talk and smile,
Whilst heavenly themes, for ever new,
    Our cares beguile.

The happy seasons oft return,
When love our melting hearts did burn,
As we through heavenly themes were borne
    With heavenward eyes,
And Faith this empty globe would spurn,
    And sail the skies.

Or, when the rising sun shines bright,
Or, setting, leaves the world in night,
Or, dazzling, sheds his noon-day light,
    Or, cloudy, hides,
My fancy, in her airy flight,
    With you resides.

Where far you wander down the vale,
When balmy scents perfume the gale,
And purling rills and linnets hail
    The King of kings,
To muse with you I never fail,
    On heavenly things.

Where dashing cataracts astound,
And foaming shake the neighbouring ground,
And spread a hoary mist around,
    With you I gaze!—
And think, amid'st the deaf'ning sound,
    On wisdom's ways.

Where rocky mountains prop the skies,
And round the smiling landscape lies,
Whilst you look down with tearful eyes
    On grovelling man,
My sympathetic fancy flies,
    The scene to scan.

From Pisgah's top we then survey
The blissful realms of endless day,
And all the short but narrow way
    That lies between,
Whilst Faith emits a heavenly ray,
    And cheers the scene.

With you I wander on the shore
To hear the angry surges roar,
Whilst foaming through the sands they pour
   With constant roll,
And meditations heavenward soar,
   And charm the soul.

On life's rough sea we're tempest-driven
In crazy barks, our canvas riven!
Such is the lot to mortals given
   Where sins resort:
But he whose anchor's fixed in heaven
   Shall gain the port.

Though swelling waves oft beat him back,
And tempests make him half a wreck,
And passions strong, with dangerous tack,
   Retard his course,
Yet Christ the pilot all will check,
   And quell their force.

So talk we as we thoughtful stray
Along the coast, where dashing spray
With rising mist o'erhangs the day,
   And wets the shore,
And thick the vivid flashes play
   And thunders roar!

Whilst passing o'er this giddy stage,
A pious and a learned sage
Resolved eternal war to wage
   With passions fell;
How oft you view with holy rage
   These imps of hell!

See! with what madd'ning force they sway
The human breast and lead astray,
Down the steep, broad, destructive way,
    The giddy throng;
Till grisly death sweeps all away
    The fiends among!

As when the mad tornado flies,
And sounding mingles earth and skies,
And wild confusion 'fore the eyes
    In terrors dressed.
So passions fell in whirlwinds rise,
    And rend the breast!

But whilst this direful tempest raves,
And many barks are dashed to staves,
I see you tower above the waves
    Like some tall rock,
Whose base the harmless ocean laves
    Without a shock!

'Tis He who calmed the raging sea,
Who bids the waves be still in thee,
And keeps you from all dangers free
    Amidst the wreck;
All sin, and care, and dangers flee
    E'en at His beck.

And on that great and dreadful day
When heaven and earth shall pass away,
Each soul to bliss He will convey,
    That knows His name;
And give the giddy world a prey
    To quenchless flame.

So oft when Sabbaths bade us rest,
And heavenly zeal inspired your breast,
Obedient to the high behest
    You preached to all,
Whilst God your zealous efforts blessed,
    And owned your call.

The very thought my soul inspires,
And kindles bright her latent fires;
My Muse feels heart-warm fond desires,
    And spreads her wing,
And aims to join th' angelic choirs,
    And sweetly sing.

May rosy Health with speed return,
And all your wonted ardour burn,
And sickness buried in his urn,
    Sleep many years!
So, countless friends who loudly mourn,
    Shall dry their tears!

Your wailing flock will all rejoice
To hear their much-loved shepherd's voice,
And long will bless the happy choice
    Their hearts have made,
And tuneful mirth will swell the noise
    Through grove and glade.

Your dearer half will join with me
To celebrate the jubilee,
And praise the Great Eternal Three
    With throbbing joy,
And taste those pleasures pure and free
    Which never cloy.

THE HAPPY COTTAGERS

One sunny morn of May,
  When dressed in flowery green
The dewy landscape, charmed
  With Nature's fairest scene,
    In thoughtful mood
    I slowly strayed
    O'er hill and dale,
      Through bush and glade.

Throughout the cloudless sky
  Of light unsullied blue,
The larks their matins raised,
  Whilst on my dizzy view,
    Like dusky motes,
      They winged their way
    Till vanished in
      The blaze of day.

The linnets sweetly sang
  On every fragrant thorn,
Whilst from the tangled wood
  The blackbirds hailed the morn;
    And through the dew
      Ran here and there,
    But half afraid,
      The startled hare.

           The balmy breeze just kissed
             The countless dewy gems
          Which decked the yielding blade
            Or gilt the sturdy stems,
              And gently o'er
                The charmed sight
              A deluge shed
                Of trembling light.

        A sympathetic glow
           Ran through my melting soul,
        And calm and sweet delight
           O'er all my senses stole;
             And through my heart
               A grateful flood
             Of joy rolled on
               To Nature's God.

        Time flew unheeded by,
           Till wearied and oppressed,
        Upon a flowery bank
           I laid me down to rest;
             Beneath my feet
               A purling stream
             Ran glittering in
               The noontide beam.

        I turned me round to view
           The lovely rural scene;
        And, just at hand, I spied
           A cottage on the green;
             The street was clean,
               The walls were white,
             The thatch was neat,
               The window bright.

Bold chanticleer, arrayed
  In velvet plumage gay,
With many an amorous dame,
  Fierce strutted o'er the way;
    And motley ducks
      Were waddling seen,
    And drake with neck
      Of glossy green.

The latch I gently raised,
  And oped the humble door;
An oaken stool was placed
  On the neat sanded floor;
    An aged man
      Said with a smile,
    "You're welcome, sir:
      Come rest a while."

His coarse attire was clean,
  His manner rude yet kind:
His air, his words, and looks
  Showed a contented mind;
    Though mean and poor,
      Thrice happy he,
    As by our tale
      You soon shall see.

But don't expect to hear
  Of deeds of martial fame,
Or that our peasant mean
  Was born of rank or name,
    And soon will strut,
      As in romance,
    A knight and all
      In armour glance.

I sing of real life;
  All else is empty show—
To those who read a source
  Of much unreal woe:
    Pollution, too,
      Through novel-veins,
    Oft fills the mind
      With guilty stains.

Our peasant long was bred
  Affliction's meagre child,
Yet gratefully resigned,
  Loud hymning praises, smiled,
    And like a tower
      He stood unmoved,
    Supported by
      The God he loved.

His loving wife long since
  Was numbered with the dead
His son, a martial youth,
  Had for his country bled;
    And now remained
      One daughter fair,
    And only she,
      To soothe his care.

The aged man with tears
  Spoke of the lovely maid;
How earnestly she strove
  To lend her father aid,
    And as he ran
      Her praises o'er,
    She gently oped
      The cottage-door.

With vegetable store
  The table soon she spread,
And pressed me to partake;
  Whilst blushes rosy-red
    Suffused her face—
      The old man smiled,
      Well pleased to see
        His darling child.

With venerable air
  He then looked up to God,
A blessing craved on all,
  And on our daily food;
    Then kindly begged
      I would excuse
      Their humble fair,
        And not refuse.—

The tablecloth, though coarse,
  Was of a snowy white,
The vessels, spoons, and knives
  Were clean and dazzling bright;
    So down we sat
      Devoid of care,
      Nor envied kings
        Their dainty fare.

When nature was refreshed,
  And we familiar grown;
The good old man exclaimed,
  "Around Jehovah's throne,
    Come, let us all
      Our voices raise,
      And sing our great
        Redeemer's praise!"

Their artless notes were sweet,
  Grace ran through every line;
Their breasts with rapture swelled,
  Their looks were all divine:
    Delight o'er all
      My senses stole,
    And heaven's pure joy
      O'erwhelmed my soul.

When we had praised our God,
  And knelt around His throne,
The aged man began
  In deep and zealous tone,
    With hands upraised
      And heavenward eye,
    And prayed loud
      And fervently:

He prayed that for His sake,
  Whose guiltless blood was shed
For guilty ruined man,
  We might that day be fed
    With that pure bread
      Which cheers the soul,
    And living stream,
      Where pleasures roll.

He prayed long for all,
  And for his daughter dear,
That she, preserved from ill,
  Might lead for many a year
    A spotless life
      When he's no more;
    Then follow him
      To Canaan's shore.

His faltering voice then fell,
  His tears were dropping fast,
And muttering praise to God
  For all His mercies past,
    He closed his prayer
      Midst heavenly joys,
    And tasted bliss
      Which never cloys.

In sweet discourse we spent
  The fast declining day:
We spoke of Jesus' love,
  And of that narrow way
    Which leads, through care
      And toil below,
    To streams where joys
      Eternal flow.

The wondrous plan of Grace,
  Adoring, we surveyed,
The birth of heavenly skill—
  In Love Eternal laid—
    Too deep for clear
      Angelic ken,
    And far beyond
      Dim-sighted men.

To tell you all that passed
  Would far exceed my power;
Suffice it, then, to say,
  Joy winged the passing hour,
    Till, ere we knew,
      The setting day
    Had clad the world
      In silver grey.

I kindly took my leave,
  And blessed the happy lot
Of those I left behind
  Lodged in their humble cot;
  And pitied some
    In palace walls,
  Where pride torments,
    And pleasure palls.

The silver moon now shed
  A flood of trembling light
On tower, and tree, and stream;
  The twinkling stars shone bright,
  Nor misty stain
    Nor cloud was seen
  O'er all the deep
    Celestial green.

Mild was the lovely night,
  Nor stirred a whispering breeze.
Smooth was the glassy lake,
  And still the leafy trees;
  No sound in air
    Was heard afloat,
  Save Philomel's
    Sweet warbling note.

My thoughts were on the wing,
  And back my fancy fled
To where contentment dwelt
  In the neat humble shed;
  To shining courts
    From thence it ran,
  Where restless pride
    Oppresses man.

In fame some search for bliss,
  Some seek content in gain,
In search of happiness
  Some give the slackened rein
    To passions fierce,
      And down the stream
    Through giddy life,
      Of pleasures dream.

These all mistake the way,
  As many more have done:
The narrow path of bliss
  Through God's Eternal Son
    Directly tends;
      And only he
    Who treads this path
      Can happy be.

Who anchors all above
  Has still a happy lot,
Though doomed for life to dwell
  E'en in a humble cot,
    And when he lays
      This covering down
    He'll wear a bright
      Immortal crown.

THE RAINBOW

The shower is past, and the sky
  O'erhead is both mild and serene,
Save where a few drops from on high,
  Like gems, twinkle over the green:
And glowing fair, in the black north,
  The rainbow o'erarches the cloud;
The sun in his glory comes forth,
  And larks sweetly warble aloud.

That dismally grim northern sky
  Says God in His vengeance once frowned,
And opened His flood-gates on high,
  Till obstinate sinners were drowned:
The lively bright south, and that bow,
  Say all this dread vengeance is o'er;
These colours that smilingly glow
  Say we shall be deluged no more.

Ever blessed be those innocent days,
  Ever sweet their remembrance to me;
When often, in silent amaze,
  Enraptured, I'd gaze upon thee!
Whilst arching adown the black sky
  Thy colours glowed on the green hill,
To catch thee as lightning I'd fly,
  But aye you eluded my skill.

From hill unto hill your gay scene
   You shifted—whilst crying aloud,
I ran, till at length from the green,
   You shifted, at once to the cloud!
So, vain worldly phantoms betray
   The youths who too eager pursue,
When ruined and far led astray,
   Th' illusion escapes from their view.

Those peaceable days knew no care,
   Except what arose from my play,
My favourite lambkin and hare,
   And cabin I built o'er the way.
No cares did I say? Ah! I'm wrong:
   Even childhood from cares is not free:
Far distant I see a grim throng
   Shake horrible lances at me!

One day—I remember it still—
   For pranks I had played on the clown
Who lived on the neighbouring hill,
   My cabin was trod to the ground.
Who ever felt grief such as I
   When crashed by this terrible blow?
Not Priam, the monarch of Troy,
   When all his proud towers lay low.

And grief upon grief was my lot:
   Soon after, my lambkin was slain;
My hare, having strayed from its cot,
   Was chased by the hounds o'er the plain.
What countless calamities teem
   From memory's page on my view!—
How trifling soever you seem,
   Yet once I have wept over you.

Then cease, foolish heart, to repine;
   No stage is exempted from care:
If you would true happiness find,
   Come follow! and I'll show you where.
But, first, let us take for our guide
   The Word which Jehovah has penned;
By this the true path is descried
   Which leads to a glorious end.

How narrow this path to our view!
   How steep an ascent lies before!
Whilst, foolish fond heart, laid for you
   Are dazzling temptations all o'er.
What bye-ways with easy descent
   Invite us through pleasures to stray!
Whilst Satan, with hellish intent,
   Suggests that we ought to obey.

But trust not the father of lies,
   He tempts you with vanity's dream;
His pleasure, when touched, quickly dies,
   Like bubbles that dance on the stream.
Look not on the wine when it glows
   All ruddy, in vessels of gold;
At last it will sting your repose,
   And death at the bottom unfold.*

But lo! an unnatural night
   Pours suddenly down on the eye;
The sun has withdrawn all his light,
   And rolls a black globe o'er the sky!
And hark! what a cry rent the air!
   Immortal the terrible sound!—
The rocks split with honible tear,
   And fearfully shakes all the ground!

---

* Proverbs xxiii. 31, 32.

The dead from their slumbers awake,
   And, leaving their mouldy domain,
Make poor guilty mortals to quake
   As pallid they glide o'er the plain!
Sure, Nature's own God is oppressed,
   And Nature in agony cries;—
The sun in his mourning is dressed,
   To tell the sad news through the skies!

Yet surely some victory's gained,
   Important, and novel, and great,
Since Death has his captives unchained,
   And widely thrown open his gate!
Yes, victory great as a God
   Could gain over hell, death, and sin,
This moment's achieved by the blood
   Of Jesus, our crucified King.

But all the dread conflict is o'er;
   Lo! cloud after cloud rolls away;
And heaven, serene as before,
   Breaks forth in the splendour of day!
And all the sweet landscape around,
   Emerged from the ocean of night,
With groves, woods, and villages crowned,
   Astonish and fill with delight!

But see! where that crowd melts away,
   Three crosses sad spectacles show!
Our Guide has not led us astray;
   Heart! this is the secret you'd know—
Two thieves, and a crucified God
   Hangs awfully mangled between!
Whilst fast from His veins spouting blood
   Runs, dyeing with purple the green!

Behold! the red flood rolls along,
   And forming a bason below,
Is termed in Emanuel's song
   The fount for uncleanness and woe.
Immerged in that precious tide,
   The soul quickly loses its stains,
Though deeper than crimson they're dyed,
   And 'scapes from its sorrows and pains.

This fountain is opened for you:
   Go, wash, without money or price;
And instantly formed anew,
   You'll lose all your woes in a trice.
Then cease, foolish heart, to repine,
   No stage is exempted from care;
If you would true happiness find,
   'Tis on Calvary—seek for it there.

WINTER-NIGHT MEDITATIONS

Rude winter's come, the sky's o'ercast,
The night is cold and loud the blast,
The mingling snow comes driving down,
Fast whitening o'er the flinty ground.
Severe their lots whose crazy sheds
Hang tottering o'er their trembling heads:
Whilst blows through walls and chinky door
The drifting snow across the floor,
Where blinking embers scarcely glow,
And rushlight only serves to show
What well may move the deepest sigh,
And force a tear from pity's eye.
You there may see a meagre pair,
Worn out with labour, grief, and care:
Whose naked babes, in hungry mood,
Complain of cold and cry for food;
Whilst tears bedew the mother's cheek,
And sighs the father's grief bespeak;
For fire or raiment, bed or board,
Their dreary shed cannot afford.

   Will no kind hand confer relief,
And wipe away the tear of grief?
A little boon it well might spare
Would kindle joy, dispel their care,
Abate the rigour of the night
And warm each heart—achievement bright.
Yea, brighter far than such as grace
The annals of a princely race,
Where kings bestow a large domain
But to receive as much again,
Or e'en corrupt the purest laws,
Or fan the breath of vain applause.

Peace to the man who stoops his head
To enter the most wretched shed:
Who, with his condescending smiles,
Poor diffidence and awe beguiles:
Till all encouraged, soon disclose
The different causes of their woes—
The moving tale dissolves his heart:
He liberally bestows a part
Of God's donation. From above
Approving Heaven, in smiles of love,
Looks on, and through the shining skies
The great Recording Angel flies
The doors of mercy to unfold,
And write the deed in lines of gold;
There, if a fruit of Faith's fair tree,
To shine throughout eternity,
In honour of that Sovereign dread,
Who had no place to lay His head,
Yet opened wide sweet Mercy's door
To all the desolate and poor,
Who, stung with guilt and hard oppressed,
Groaned to be with Him, and at rest.

   Now, pent within the city wall,
They throng to theatre and hall,
Where gesture, look, and words conspire,
To stain the mind, the passions fire;
Whence sin-polluted streams abound,
That whelm the country all around.
Ah! Modesty, should you be here,
Close up the eye and stop the ear;
Oppose your fan, nor peep beneath,
And blushing shun their tainted breath.

   Here every rake exerts his art
T' ensnare the unsuspecting heart.
The prostitute, with faithless smiles,
Remorseless plays her tricks and wiles.
Her gesture bold and ogling eye,
Obtrusive speech and pert reply,

And brazen front and stubborn tone,
Show all her native virtue's flown.
By her the thoughtless youth is ta'en,
Impoverished, disgraced, or slain:
Through her the marriage vows are broke,
And Hymen proves a galling yoke.
Diseases come, destruction's dealt,
Where'er her poisonous breath is felt;
Whilst she, poor wretch, dies in the flame
That runs through her polluted frame.

  Once she was gentle, fair, and kind,
To no seducing schemes inclined,
Would blush to hear a smutty tale,
Nor ever strolled o'er hill or dale,
But lived a sweet domestic maid,
To lend her aged parents aid—
And oft they gazed and oft they smiled
On this their loved and only child:
They thought they might in her be blest,
And she would see them laid at rest.

  A blithesome youth of courtly mien
Oft called to see this rural queen:
His oily tongue and wily art
Soon gained Maria's yielding heart.
The aged pair, too, liked the youth,
And thought him naught but love and truth.
The village feast at length is come;
Maria by the youth's undone:
The youth is gone—so is her fame;
And with it all her sense of shame:
And now she practises the art
Which snared her unsuspecting heart;
And vice, with a progressive sway,
More hardened makes her every day.
Averse to good and prone to ill,
And dexterous in seducing skill;
To look, as if her eyes would melt:
T' affect a love she never felt;

To half suppress the rising sigh;
Mechanically to weep and cry;
To vow eternal truth, and then
To break her vow, and vow again;
Her ways are darkness, death, and hell:
Remorse and shame and passions fell,
And short-lived joy, with endless pain,
Pursues her in a gloomy train.

  O Britain fair, thou queen of isles!
Nor hostile arms nor hostile wiles
Could ever shake thy solid throne
But for thy sins. Thy sins alone
Can make thee stoop thy royal head,
And lay thee prostrate with the dead.
In vain colossal England mows,
With ponderous strength, the yielding foes;
  In vain fair Scotia, by her side,
With courage flushed and Highland pride,
Whirls her keen blade with horrid whistle
And lops off heads like tops of thistle;
In vain brave Erin, famed afar,
The flaming thunderbolt of war,
Profuse of life, through blood does wade,
To lend her sister kingdom aid:
Our conquering thunders vainly roar
Terrific round the Gallic shore;
Profoundest statesmen vainly scheme—
'Tis all a vain, delusive dream,
If treacherously within our breast
We foster sin, the deadly pest.

  Where Sin abounds Religion dies,
And Virtue seeks her native skies;
Chaste Conscience hides for very shame,
And Honour's but an empty name.
Then, like a flood, with fearful din,
A gloomy host comes pouring in.

First Bribery, with her golden shield,
Leads smooth Corruption o'er the field;
Dissension wild, with brandished spear,
And Anarchy bring up the rear:
Whilst Care and Sorrow, Grief and Pain
Run howling o'er the bloody plain.

O Thou, whose power resistless fills
The boundless whole, avert those ills
We richly merit: purge away
The sins which on our vitals prey;
Protect, with Thine almighty shield
Our conquering arms by flood and field,
Wheel round the time when Peace shall smile
O'er Britain's highly-favoured Isle;
When all shall loud hosannas sing
To Thee, the great Eternal King!

   But hark! the bleak, loud whistling wind!
Its crushing blast recalls to mind
The dangers of the troubled deep;
Where, with a fierce and thundering sweep,
The winds in wild distraction rave,
And push along the mountain wave
With dreadful swell and hideous curl!
Whilst hung aloft in giddy whirl,
Or drop beneath the ocean's bed,
The leaky bark without a shred
Of rigging sweeps through dangers dread.
The flaring beacon points the way,
And fast the pumps loud clanking play:
It 'vails not—hark! with crashing shock
She's shivered 'gainst the solid rock,
Or by the fierce, incessant waves
Is beaten to a thousand staves;
Or bilging at her crazy side,
Admits the thundering hostile tide,
And down she sinks!—triumphant rave
The winds, and close her wat'ry grave!

The merchant's care and toil are vain,
His hopes He buried in the main—
In vain the mother's tearful eye
Looks for its sole remaining joy—
In vain fair Susan walks the shore,
And sighs for him she'll see no more—
For deep they lie in ocean's womb,
And fester in a wat'ry tomb.

Now, from the frothy, thundering main,
My meditations seek the plain,
Where, with a swift fantastic flight,
They scour the regions of the night,
Free as the winds that wildly blow
O'er hill and dale the blinding snow,
Or, through the woods, their frolics play,
And whirling, sweep the dusty way,
When summer shines with burning glare,
And sportive breezes skim the air,
And Ocean's glassy breast is fanned
To softest curl by Zephyr bland.

But Summer's gone, and Winter's here—
With iron sceptre rules the year—
Beneath this dark inclement sky
How many wanderers faint and die!
One, flouncing o'er the treacherous snow,
Sinks in the pit that yawns below!
Another numbed, with panting lift
Inhales the suffocating drift!
And creeping cold, with stiffening force,
Extends a third, a pallid corse!

Thus death, in varied dreadful form,
Triumphant rides along the storm:
With shocking scenes assails the sight,
And makes more sad the dismal night!
How blest the man, whose lot is free
From such distress and misery;

WINTER-NIGHT MEDITATIONS

Who, sitting by his blazing fire,
Is closely wrapt in warm attire;
Whose sparkling glasses blush with wine
Of mirthful might and flavour fine;
Whose house, compact and strong, defies
The rigour of the angry skies!
The ruffling winds may blow their last,
And snows come driving on the blast;
And frosts their icy morsels fling,
But all within is mild as spring!

How blest is he!—blest did I say?
E'en sorrow here oft finds its way.
The senses numbed by frequent use,
Of criminal, absurd abuse
Of heaven's blessings, listless grow,
And life is but a dream of woe.

Oft fostered on the lap of ease,
Grow racking pain and foul disease,
And nervous whims, a ghastly train,
Inflicting more than corp'ral pain:
Oft gold and shining pedigree
Prove only splendid misery.
The king who sits upon his throne,
And calls the kneeling world his own,
Has oft of cares a greater load
Than he who feels his iron rod.

No state is free from care and pain
Where fiery passions get the rein,
Or soft indulgence, joined with ease,
Begets a thousand ills to tease:
Where fair Religion, heavenly maid,
Has slighted still her offered aid.
Her matchless power the will subdues,
And gives the judgment clearer views:
Denies no source of real pleasure,
And yields us blessings out of measure;

Our prospect brightens, proves our stay,
December turns to smiling May;
Conveys us to that peaceful shore,
By raging billows lashed no more,
Where endless happiness remains,
And one eternal summer reigns.

VERSES SENT TO A LADY ON HER BIRTHDAY

The joyous day illumes the sky
That bids each care and sorrow fly
    To shades of endless night:
E'en frozen age, thawed in the fires
Of social mirth, feels young desires,
    And tastes of fresh delight.

In thoughtful mood your parents dear,
Whilst joy smiles through the starting tear,
    Give approbation due.
As each drinks deep in mirthful wine
Your rosy health, and looks benign
    Are sent to heaven for you.

But let me whisper, lovely fair,
This joy may soon give place to care,
    And sorrow cloud this day;
Full soon your eyes of sparkling blue,
And velvet lips of scarlet hue,
    Discoloured, may decay.

As bloody drops on virgin snows,
So vies the lily with the rose
    Full on your dimpled cheek;
But ah! the worm in lazy coil
May soon prey on this putrid spoil,
    Or leap in loathsome freak.

Fond wooers come with flattering tale,
And load with sighs the passing gale,
   And love-distracted rave:
But hark, fair maid! whate'er they say,
You're but a breathing mass of clay,
   Fast ripening for the grave.

Behold how thievish Time has been!
Full eighteen summers you have seen,
   And yet they seem a day?
Whole years, collected in Time's glass,
In silent lapse how soon they pass,
   And steal your life away!

The flying hour none can arrest,
Nor yet recall one moment past,
   And what more dread must seem
Is, that to-morrow's not your own—
Then haste! and ere your life has flown
   The subtle hours redeem.

Attend with care to what I sing:
Know time is ever on the wing;
   None can its flight detain;
Then, like a pilgrim passing by,
Take home this hint, as time does fly,
   "All earthly things are vain."

Let nothing here elate your breast,
Nor, for one moment, break your rest,
   In heavenly wisdom grow:
Still keep your anchor fixed above,
Where Jesus reigns in boundless love,
   And streams of pleasure flow.

So shall your life glide smoothly by
Without a tear, without a sigh,
    And purest joys will crown
Each birthday, as the year revolves,
Till this clay tenement dissolves,
    And leaves the soul unbound.

Then shall you land on Canaan's shore,
Where time and chance shall be no more,
    And joy eternal reigns;
There, mixing with the seraphs bright,
And dressed in robes of heavenly light,
    You'll raise angelic strains.

THE IRISH CABIN

Should poverty, modest and clean,
   E'er please, when presented to view,
Should cabin on brown heath, or green,
   Disclose aught engaging to you,
Should Erin's wild harp soothe the ear
   When touched by such fingers as mine,
Then kindly attentive draw near,
   And candidly ponder each line.

One day, when December's keen breath
   Arrested the sweet running rill,
And Nature seemed frozen in death,
   I thoughtfully strolled o'er the hill:
The mustering clouds wore a frown,
   The mountains were covered with snow,
And Winter his mantle of brown
   Had spread o'er the landscape below.

Thick rattling the footsteps were heard
   Of peasants far down in the vale;
From lakes, bogs, and marshes debarred,
   The wild-fowl, aloft on the gale,
Loud gabbling and screaming were borne,
   Whilst thundering guns hailed the day,
And hares sought the thicket forlorn,
   Or, wounded, ran over the way.

THE IRISH CABIN

No music was heard in the grove,
   The blackbird and linnet and thrush,
And goldfinch and sweet cooing dove,
   Sat pensively mute in the bush:
The leaves that once wove a green shade
   Lay withered in heaps on the ground:
Chill Winter through grove, wood, and glade
   Spread sad desolation around.

But now the keen north wind 'gan whistle,
   And gusty, swept over the sky;
Each hair, frozen, stood like a bristle,
   And night thickened fast on the eye.
In swift-wheeling eddies the snow
   Fell, mingling and drifting amain,
And soon all distinction laid low,
   As whitening it covered the plain.

A light its pale ray faintly shot
   (The snow-flakes its splendour had shorn),
It came from a neighbouring cot,
   Some called it the Cabin of Mourne:*
A neat Irish Cabin, snow-proof,
   Well thatched, had a good earthen floor,
One chimney in midst of the roof,
   One window, and one latched door.

Escaped from the pitiless storm,
   I entcred the humble retreat;
Compact was the building, and warm,
   Its furniture simple and neat.
And now, gentle reader, approve
   The ardour that glowed in each breast,
As kindly our cottagers strove
   To cherish and welcome their guest.

---

  * Mourne consists chiefly of a range of high mountains in the north of Ireland

The dame nimbly rose from her wheel,
   And brushed off the powdery snow:
Her daughter, forsaking the reel,
   Ran briskly the cinders to blow:
The children, who sat on the hearth,
   Leaped up without murmur or frown,
An oaken stool quickly brought forth,
   And smilingly bade me sit down.

Whilst grateful sensations of joy
   O'er all my fond bosom were poured,
Resumed was each former employ,
   And gay thrifty order restored:
The blaze flickered up to the crook,
   The reel clicked again by the door,
The dame turned her wheel in the nook,
   And frisked the sweet babes round the floor.

Released from the toils of the barn,
   His thrifty, blithe wife hailed the sire,
And hanging his flail by her yarn,
   He drew up his stool to the fire;
Then smoothing his brow with his hand,
   As if he would sweep away sorrow,
He says, "Let us keep God's command,
   And never take thought for the morrow."

Brisk turning him round with a smile,
   And freedom unblended by art,
And affable manners and style,
   Though simple, that reached to my heart,
He said (whilst with ardour he glowed),
   "Kind sir, we are poor, yet we're blest:
We're all in the steep, narrow road
   That leads to the city of rest.

"'Tis true, I must toil all the day,
  And oft suffer cold through the night,
Though silvered all over with grey,
  And dimly declining my sight:
And sometimes our raiment and food
  Are scanty—ah! scanty indeed:
But all work together for good,
  So in my blest Bible I read.

"I also have seen in that Book
  (Perhaps you can tell me the place?)
How God on poor sinners does look
  In pity, and gives them His grace—
Yea, gives them His grace in vast store,
  Sufficient to help them quite through,
Though troubles should whelm them all o'er;
  And sure this sweet promise is true!

"Yes, true as the snow blows without,
  And winds whistle keen through the air,
His grace can remove every doubt,
  And chase the black gloom of despair:
It often supports my weak mind,
  And wipes the salt tear from my eye,
It tells me that Jesus is kind,
  And died for such sinners as I.

"I once rolled in wealth, without grace,
  But happiness ne'er was my lot,
Till Christ freely pitied my case,
  And now I am blest in a cot:
Well knowing things earthly are vain,
  Their troubles ne'er puzzle my head;
Convinced that to die will be gain,
  I look on the grave as my bed.

"I look on the grave as my bed,
   Where I'll sleep the swift hours away,
Till waked from their slumbers, the dead
   Shall rise, never more to decay:
Then I, with my children and wife,
   Shall get a bright palace above,
And endlessly clothed with life,
   Shall dwell in the Eden of love.

"Then know, gentle stranger, though poor,
   We're cheerful, contented, and blest;
Though princes should pass by our door
   King Jesus is ever our guest;
We feel, and we taste, and we see
   The pleasures which flow from our Lord,
And fearless, and wealthy, and free,
   We live on the joys of His word."

He ceased: and a big tear of joy
   Rolled glittering down to the ground;
Whilst all, having dropped their employ,
   Were buried in silence profound;
A sweet, solemn pause long ensued—
   Each bosom o'erflowed with delight;
Then heavenly converse renewed,
   Beguiled the dull season of night.

We talked of the rough narrow way
   That leads to the kingdom of rest;
On Pisgah we stood to survey
   The King in His holiness dressed—
Even Jesus, the crucified King,
   Whose blood in rich crimson does flow,
Clean washing the crimson of sin,
   And rinsing it whiter that snow.[*]

---

[*] Isaiah i. 18.

But later and later it's wearing,
  And supper they cheerfully bring,
The mealy potato and herring,
  And water just fresh from the spring.
They press, and they smile: we sit down;
  First praying the Father of Love
Our table with blessings to crown,
  And feed us with bread from above.

The wealthy and bloated may sneer,
  And sicken o'er luxury's dishes,
And loathe the poor cottager's cheer,
  And melt in the heat of their wishes:
But luxury's sons are unblest,
  A prey to each giddy desire,
And hence, where they never know rest,
  They sink in unquenchable fire.

Not so, the poor cottager's lot,
  Who travels the Zion-ward road,
He's blest in his neat little cot,
  He's rich in the favour of God;
By faith he surmounts every wave
  That rolls on this sea of distress:
Triumphant, he dives in the grave,
  To rise on the ocean of bliss.

Now supper is o'er and we raise
  Our prayers to the Father of light
And joyfully hymning His praise,
  We lovingly bid a good-night.—
The ground's white, the sky's cloudless blue,
  The breeze flutters keen through the air,
The stars twinkle bright on my view,
  As I to my mansion repair.

All peace, my dear cottage, be thine!
  Nor think that I'll treat you with scorn;
Whoever reads verses of mine
  Shall hear of the Cabin of Mourne;
And had I but musical strains,
  Though humble and mean in your station
You should smile whilst the world remains,
  The pride of the fair Irish Nation.

In friendship, fair Erin, you glow;
  Offended, you quickly forgive;
Your courage is known to each foe,
  Yet foes on your bounty might live.
Some faults you, however, must own;
  Dissensions, impetuous zeal,
And wild prodigality, grown
  Too big for your income and weal.

Ah! Erin, if you would be great,
  And happy, and wealthy, and wise,
And trample your sorrows, elate,
  Contend for our cottager's prize;
So error and vice shall decay,
  And concord add bliss to renown,
And you shall gleam brighter than day,
  The gem of the fair British Crown.

TO THE REV. J. GILPIN

ON HIS IMPROVED EDITION OF THE "PILGRIM'S PROGRESS."

When, Reverend Sir, your good design,
To clothe our Pilgrim gravely fine,
And give him gentler mien and gait,
First reached my ear, his doubtful fate
With dread suspense my mind oppressed,
Awoke my fears, and broke my rest.
Yet, still, had England said, "You're free,
Choose whom you will," dear sir, to thee,
For dress beseeming modest worth,
I would have led our pilgrim forth.

  But when I viewed him o'er and o'er,
And scrutinized the weeds he wore,
And marked his mien and marked his gait,
And saw him trample sin, elate,
And heard him speak, though coarse and plain,
His mighty truths in nervous strain,
I could not gain my own consent
To your acknowledged good intent.

  I had my fears, lest honest John,
When he beheld his polished son
(If saints ought earthly care to know),
Would take him for some Bond Street beau,
Or for that thing—it wants a name—
Devoid of truth, of sense and shame,
Which smooths its chin and licks its lip,
And mounts the pulpit with a skip,
Then turning round its pretty face,
To smite each fair one in the place,
Relaxes half to vacant smile,

    And aims with trope and polished style,
And lisp affected, to pourtray
Its silly self in colours gay—
Its fusty moral stuff t' unload,
And preach itself, and not its God.
Thus, wishing, doubting, trembling led,
I oped your book, your Pilgrim read.

    As rising Phœbus lights the skies,
And fading night before him flies,
Till darkness to his cave is hurled
And golden day has gilt the world,
Nor vapour, cloud, nor mist is seen
To sully all the pure serene:
So, as I read each modest line,
Increasing light began to shine,
My cloudy fears and doubts gave way,
Till all around shone Heaven's own day.

    And when I closed the book, thought I,
Should Bunyan leave his throne on high;
He'd own the kindness you have done
To Christian, his orphan son:
And smiling as once Eden smiled,
Would thus address his holy child:—

    "My son, ere I removed from hence,
I spared nor labour nor expense
To gain for you the heavenly prize,
And teach you to make others wise.
But still, though inward worth was thine,
You lay a diamond in the mine:
You wanted outward polish bright
To show your pure intrinsic light.
Some knew your worth, and seized the prize,
And now are thronèd in the skies:
Whilst others swilled with folly's wine,
But trod the pearl like the swine,
In ignorance sunk in their grave,
And thence, where burning oceans lave.

Now polished bright, your native flame
And inward worth are still the same;
A flaming diamond still you glow,
In brighter hues: then cheery go—
More suited by a skilful hand
To do your father's high command:
Fit ornament for sage or clown,
Or beggar's rags, or kingly crown.

THE COTTAGE MAID

Aloft on the brow of a mountain,
And hard by a clear running fountain,
   In neat little cot,
   Content with her lot,
Retired, there lives a sweet maiden.

Her father is dead, and her brother—
And now she alone with her mother
   Will spin on her wheel,
   And sew, knit, and reel,
And cheerfully work for their living.

To gossip she never will roam,
She loves, and she stays at, her home,
   Unless when a neighbour
   In sickness does labour,
Then, kindly, she pays her a visit.

With Bible she stands by her bed,
And when some blest passage is read,
   In prayer and in praises
   Her sweet voice she raises
To Him who for sinners once died.

Well versed in her Bible is she,
Her language is artless and free,
   Imparting pure joy,
   That never can cloy,
And smoothing the pillow of death.

To novels and plays not inclined,
Nor aught that can sully her mind;
    Temptations may shower,—
    Unmoved as a tower,
She quenches the fiery arrows.

She dresses as plain as the lily
That modestly glows in the valley,
    And never will go
    To play, dance or show—
She calls them the engines of Satan.

With tears in her eyes she oft says,
"Away with your dances and plays!
    The ills that perplex
    The half of our sex
Are owing to you, Satan's engines."

Released from her daily employment,
Intent upon solid enjoyment,
    Her time she won't idle,
    But reads in her Bible,
And books that divinely enlighten.

Whilst others at wake, dance, and play
Chide life's restless moments away,
    And ruin their souls—
    In pleasure she rolls,
The foretaste of heavenly joys.

Her soul is refined by her Lord,
She shines in the truths of His Word:
    Each Christian grace
    Shines full in her face,
And heightens the glow of her charms.

One day as I passed o'er the mountain,
She sung by a clear crystal fountain
   (Nor knew I was near);
   Her notes charmed my ear,
As thus she melodiously chanted:

"Oh! when shall we see our dear Jesus?
His presence from poverty frees us,—
   And bright from His face
   The rays of His grace
Beam, purging transgression for ever.

"Oh! when shall we see our dear Jesus?
His presence from sorrow will ease us,
   When up to the sky
   With angels we fly—
Then farewell all sorrow for ever!

"Come quickly! come quickly, Lord Jesus!
Thy presence alone can appease us;
   For aye on Thy breast
   Believers shall rest,
Where blest they shall praise Thee for ever."

Oh, had you but seen this sweet maiden!
She smiled like the flowers of Eden,
   And raised to the skies
   Her fond beaming eyes,
And sighed to be with her Redeemer

While thus she stood heavenly musing,
And sometimes her Bible perusing,
   Came over the way,
   All silvered with grey,
A crippled and aged poor woman.

THE COTTAGE MAID

Her visage was sallow and thin,
Through her rags peeped her sunburnt skin;
    With sorrow oppressed,
    She held to her breast
An infant, all pallid with hunger.

Half breathless by climbing the mountain,
She tremblingly stood by the fountain,
    And begged that our maid
    Would lend her some aid,
And pity both her and her infant.

Our maiden had nought but her earning—
Her heart with soft pity was yearning;
    She drooped like a lily
    Bedewed in the valley,
Whilst tears fell in pearly showers.

With air unaffected and winning,
To cover them, of her own spinning
    Her apron of blue,
    Though handsome and new,
She gave, and led them to her cottage.

All peace, my dear maiden, be thine:
Your manners and looks are divine;
    On earth you shall rest,
    In heaven be blest,
And shine like an angel for ever.

More blest than the king on the throne
Is he who shall call you his own!
    The ruby, with you
    Compared, fades to blue—
Its price is but dust on the balance.*

---

* Proverbs xxxi. 10.

Religion makes beauty enchanting,
And even where beauty is wanting,
   The temper and mind,
    Religion-refined,
Will shine through the veil with sweet lustre.

THE SPIDER AND THE FLY

The sun shines bright, the morning's fair,
The gossamers* float on the air,
The dew-gems twinkle in the glare,
    The spider's loom
Is closely plied, with artful care,
    Even in my room.

See how she moves in zigzag line,
And draws along her silken twine,
Too soft for touch, for sight too fine,
    Nicely cementing:
And makes her polished drapery shine,
    The edge indenting.

Her silken ware is gaily spread,
And now she weaves herself a bed,
Where, hiding all but just her head,
    She watching lies
For moths or gnats, entangled spread,
    Or buzzing flies.

You cunning pest! why, forward, dare
So near to lay your bloody snare!
But you to kingly courts repair
    With fell design,
And spread with kindred courtiers there
    Entangling twine.†

---

* Gossamers are the fine down of plants or the slender threads of insects, which are frequently seen to glide through the sunny atmosphere.

† Proverbs xxx. 28.

Ah, silly fly! will you advance?
I see you in the sunbeam dance:
Attracted by the silken glance
    In that dread loom;
Or blindly led, by fatal chance,
    To meet your doom.

Ah! think not, 'tis the velvet flue
Of hare, or rabbit, tempts your view;
Or silken threads of dazzling hue,
    To ease your wing,
The foaming savage, couched for you,
    Is on the spring.

Entangled! freed!—and yet again
You touch! 'tis o'er—that plaintive strain,
That mournful buzz, that struggle vain,
    Proclaim your doom:
Up to the murderous den you're ta'en,
    Your bloody tomb!

So thoughtless youths will trifling play
With dangers on their giddy way,
Or madly err in open day
    Through passions fell,
And fall, though warned oft, a prey
    To death and hell!

But hark! the fluttering leafy trees
Proclaim the gently swelling breeze,
Whilst through my window, by degrees,
    Its breathings play:
The spider's web, all tattered flees,
    Like thought, away.

Thus worldlings lean on broken props,
And idly weave their cobweb-hopes,
And hang o'er hell by spider's ropes,
    Whilst sins enthral;
Affliction blows—their joy elopes—
    And down they fall!*

---

* Job viii. 13, 14.

EPISTLE TO A YOUNG CLERGYMAN

"Study to show thyself approved unto God, a workman that needeth not to be ashamed, rightly dividing the word of truth."—2 Timothy ii. 15.

My youthful brother, oft I long
To write to you in prose or song;
With no pretence to judgment strong,
    But warm affection—
May truest friendship rivet long
    Our close connection!

With deference, what I impart
Receive with humble grateful heart,
Nor proudly from my counsel start,
    I only lend it—
A friend ne'er aims a poisoned dart—
    He wounds, to mend it.

A graduate you've just been made,
And lately passed the Mitred Head;
I trust, by the Blest Spirit, led,
    And Shepherd's care:
And not a wolf, in sheepskin clad,
    As numbers are.

The greatest office you sustain
For love of souls, and not of gain:
Through your neglect should one be slain,
    The Scriptures say,
Your careless hands his blood will stain,
    On the Last Day.

But if pure truths, like virgin snows,
You loud proclaim, to friends and foes,
Consoling these, deterring those—
    To heaven you'll fly;
Though stubborn sinners still oppose,
    And graceless die.*

Divide the word of truth aright,
Show Jesus in a saving light,
Proclaim to all they're dead outright
    Till Grace restore them:†
The great Redeemer, full in sight,
    Keep still before them.

Dare not, like some, to mince the matter—
Nor dazzling tropes and figures scatter,
Nor coarsely speak nor basely flatter,
    Nor grovelling go:
But let plain truths, as Life's pure water,
    Pellucid flow.

The sinner level with the dead,
The Lamb exalt, the Church's Head,
His holiness, adoring spread,
    With godly zeal:
Enforce, though sinless, how He bled
    For sinners' weal.

Pourtray how God in thunder spoke
His fiery Law, whilst curling smoke,
In terror fierce, from Sinai broke,
    Midst raging flame!
Then Jesu's milder blood invoke,
    And preach His name.

---

* Ezek. xxxiii. 8, 9.

† Ephes. ii. 1-8.

Remember still to fear the Lord,
To live, as well as preach, His word,
And wield the Gospel's two-edged sword,
    Though dangers lower—
Example only can afford
    To precept power.

And dress nor slovenly nor gay,
Nor sternly act; nor trifling play;
Still keep the golden middle way
    Whate'er betide you;
And ne'er through giddy pleasures stray,
    Though fools deride you.

As wily serpent ever prove,
Yet harmless as the turtle-dove,
Still winning souls by guileful love
    And deep invention—
So once the great Apostle strove
    With good intention.*

And inly to thyself take heed,
Oft prove your heart, its pages read,—
Self-knowledge will, in time of need,
    Your wants supply;
Who knows himself, from dangers freed,
    Where'er he lie.

So God will own the labours done,
Approving see His honoured Son,
And honoured Law; and numbers won
    Of souls immortal,
Through grace, will onward conquering run
    To heaven's bright portal.

---

* St Paul, 2 Cor. xii. 16.

And on that last and greatest day,
When heaven and earth shall pass away,
A perfect band, in bright array,
    Will form your crown,
Your joys triumphant wide display,
    And sorrows drown.

And now farewell, my youthful friend—
Excuse these lines, in candour penned;
To me as freely counsel lend,
    With zeal as fervent—
For you will pray, till life does end,
    Your humble servant.

EPISTLE TO THE LABOURING POOR

All you who turn the sturdy soil,
Or ply the loom with daily toil,
And lowly on through life turmoil
    For scanty fare,
Attend, and gather richest spoil
    To soothe your care.

I write with tender, feeling heart—
Then kindly read what I impart;
'Tis freely penned, devoid of art,
    In homely style,
'Tis meant to ward off Satan's dart,
    And show his guile.

I write to ope your sin-closed eyes,
And make you great, and rich, and wise,
And give you peace when trials rise,
    And sorrows gloom;
I write to fit you for the skies
    On Day of Doom.

What, though you dwell in lowly cot,
And share through life a humble lot?
Some thousands wealth and fame have got,
    Yet know no rest:
They build, pull down, and scheme and plot,
    And die unblest.

EPISTLE TO THE LABOURING POOR

Your mean attire and scanty fare
Are, doubtless, springs of bitter care—
Expose you blushing, trembling, bare,
    To haughty scorn;
Yet murmur not in black despair,
    Nor weep forlorn.

You see that lordling glittering ride
In all the pomp of wealth and pride,
With lady lolling at his side,
    And train attendant:
'Tis all, when felt and fairly tried,
    But care resplendent.

As riches grow his wants increase,
His passions burn and gnaw his peace,
Ambition foams like raging seas
    And breaks the rein,
Excess produces pale disease
    And racking pain.

Compared with him thrice happy you;
Though small your stock your wants are few—
Each wild desire your toils subdue,
    And sweeten rest,
Remove all fancied ills from view,
    And calm your breast.

Your labours give the coarsest food
A relish sweet and cleanse the blood,
Make cheerful health in spring-tide flood
    Incessant boil,
And seldom restless thoughts obtrude
    On daily toil.

Those relish least who proudly own
Rich groves and parks familiar grown;
The gazing stranger passing on
    Enjoys them most—
The toy possessed—the pleasure's flown,
    For ever lost.

Then grateful let each murmur die,
And joyous wipe the tearful eye:
Erect a palace in the sky—
    Be rich in grace:
Loathe this vain world, and longing sigh
    For Jesu's face.

Both rich and poor, who serve not God,
But live in sin, averse to good,
Rejecting Christ's atoning blood,
    Midst hellish shoals,
Shall welter in that fiery flood,
    Which hissing rolls.

But all who worship God aright,
In Christ His Son and image bright,
With minds illumed by Gospel light,
    Shall find the way
That leads to bliss, and take their flight
    To heavenly day.

There rich and poor, and high and low,
Nor sin, nor pain, nor sorrow know:
There Christ with one eternal glow
    Gives life and light—
There streams of pleasure ever flow,
    And pure delight.

Christ says to all with sin oppressed,
"Come here, and taste of heavenly rest,
Receive Me as your friendly guest
    Into your cots;
In Me you shall be rich and blest,
    Though mean your lots.

"Behold My hands, My feet, My side,
All crimsoned with the bloody tide!
For you I wept, and bled, and died,
    And rose again:
And thronèd at My Father's side,
    Now plead amain!

"Repent, and enter Mercy's door,
And though you dwell in cots obscure,
All guilty, ragged, hungry, poor,
    I give in love
A crown of gold, and pardon sure,
    To each above."

Then hear the kind, inviting voice—
Believing in the Lord rejoice;
Your souls will hymn the happy choice
    To God on high,
Whilst joyful angels swell the noise
    Throughout the sky.

A fond farewell!—each cottage friend,
To Jesu's love I would commend
Your souls and bodies to the end
    Of life's rough way;
Then (death subdued) may you ascend
    To endless day!

THE COTTAGER'S HYMN

I.

My food is but spare,
  And humble my cot,
Yet Jesus dwells there
  And blesses my lot:
Though thinly I'm clad,
  And tempests oft roll,
He's raiment, and bread,
  And drink to my soul.

II.

His presence is wealth,
  His grace is a treasure,
His promise is health
  And joy out of measure.
His word is my rest,
  His spirit my guide:
In Him I am blest
  Whatever betide.

III.

Since Jesus is mine,
   Adieu to all sorrow;
I ne'er shall repine,
   Nor think of to-morrow:
The lily so fair,
   And raven so black,
He nurses with care,
   Then how shall I lack?

IV.

Each promise is sure,
   That shines in His word,
And tells me, though poor,
   I'm rich in my Lord.
Hence! Sorrow and Fear!
   Since Jesus is nigh,
I'll dry up each tear
   And stifle each sigh.

V.

Though prince, duke, or lord,
   Ne'er enter my shed,
King Jesus my board
   With dainties does spread.
Since He is my guest,
   For joy I shall sing,
And ever be blest
   In Jesus my King.

VI.

With horrible din
  Afflictions may swell,—
They cleanse me from sin,
  They save me from hell:
They're all but the rod
  Of Jesus, in love;
They lead me to God
  And blessings above.

VII.

Through sickness and pain
  I flee to my Lord,
Sweet comfort to gain,
  And health from His word;
Bleak scarcities raise
  A keener desire,
To feed on His grace,
  And wear His attire.

VIII.

The trials which frown,
  Applied by His blood,
But plait me a crown,
  And work for my good.
In praise I shall tell,
  When throned in my rest,
The things which befell
  Were always the best.

IX.

Whatever is hid
  Shall burst on my sight
When hence I have fled
  To glorious light.
Should chastisements lower,
  Then let me resign;
Should kindnesses shower,
  Let gratitude shine.

X.

Hence! Sorrow and Fear!
  Since Jesus is nigh,
I'll dry up each tear,
  And stifle each sigh:
And clothed in His word
  Will conquer my foes,
And follow my Lord
  Wherever He goes.

XI.

My friends! let us fly
  To Jesus our King;
And still as we hie,
  Of grace let us sing.
Through pleasure and pain,
  If faithful we prove,
For cots we shall gain
  A palace above.

www.ingramcontent.com/pod-product-compliance
Ingram Content Group UK Ltd.
Pitfield, Milton Keynes, MK11 3LW, UK
UKHW041303180426
11947UKWH00009B/648